Praise for My...

"Aiden Shaw, one clever hot house flow.., ..., ... honest glimpse into a world very few experience first hand in his steamy autobiography. I couldn't put it down."

—Todd Oldham

"A bittersweet triumph. The sex, drugs, and thrill seeking are just the trimmings around the real crux of the story: Shaw's ongoing quest for true love. He's the only one I know who can tug at your heartstrings and your crotch at the same time."

—Michael Musto

"Aiden Shaw tells the truth, and the truth sometimes hurts. But he tells the most truth about himself."

—Chi Chi LaRue

"It's a story for everyone. It's everyone's story. Forevermore I will associate Aiden with light. Silver light. The light outside my window at 5 a.m. as I finished his book, which I started at midnight."

—Pete Burns

Praise for *Wasted*

"Aiden Shaw is a 'crash course for the ravers,' a living, breathing, shitting, pissing contradiction who could charm your granny or bring the fear of God to a darkroom. His writing takes us to places some of us have been and never want to go to again, or where some may never want to go in the first place. It's hard to imagine anything that Shaw has not already experienced, swallowed or survived and as you read this latest tome you will probably experience flashbacks, hear deliciously dark beats and be reacquainted with some of your darkest thoughts. In real life Aiden Shaw is a true survivor but on the page he provides no happy endings and the gay underground his characters inhabit is far from fluffy or apologetic. He delivers his tale of chemical indulgence, sexual depravity, sexual abuse and cuddles with unnerving knowingness and you feel you know some of the characters a little more than you'd like too, or would like to admit. *Wasted* is dripping with uncomfortable lust that makes you sit up and squirm at times and nothing ever turns out the way you want or hope it will. Read it and weep!"

—Boy George

"Aiden Shaw has written the kind of book my mother warned me about. I tried to put it down but it stuck to my hand."

—Justin Bond (Kiki of Kiki and Herb)

"Aiden Shaw is the John Rechy of his generation. From sexual outlaw to renowned porn star to exceptional author, his transformation is complete."

—Marc Almond

"He has a gift for comedy and real clarity. He leaves our cracked and broken world beautifully, pleasingly cracked and broken in his honest, intelligent prose."

—Matthew Stadler, author of *Allan Stein*

Sordid
Truths

AIDEN SHAW

Sordid Truths

SELLING MY INNOCENCE
FOR A TASTE OF STARDOM

ALYSON books

Sordid Truths
Selling My Innocence for a Taste of Stardom

Copyright © 2009 by Aiden Shaw

Published by Alyson Books
245 West 17th Street, Suite 1200, New York, NY 10011

ALYSON books

First Alyson Books editon: November 2009

Library of Congress Cataloging-in-Publication data are on file.

ISBN-10: 1-59350-137-4
ISBN-13: 978-1-59350-137-2

10 9 8 7 6 5 4 3 2 1

Cover design by Nick Vogelson
Cover photo copyright © by Mark Beard
Interior design by Maria Fernandez, Neuwirth & Associates, Inc.

Printed in the United States of America
Distributed by Consortium Book Sales and Distribution
Distribution in the United Kingdom by Turnaround Publisher Services Ltd

This book is dedicated to

The grown-ups who misguided me. The teachers that tried to trick me. The religions that abused my faith. The lovers that hated me. Everybody who put me down or enjoyed embarrassing me. To all the things in my life that hurt me and gave me cause.

"To believe your own thought, to believe that what is true for you in your private heart is true for all—that is genius."
—Ralph Waldo Emerson (1803–1882)

ACKNOWLEDGMENTS

I'd like to thank firstly, and probably most importantly, everybody who is in or inspired this book. On a more practical note, and without whom this would have been a very different, lesser book, my editor and right-hand man, Patrick Merla. My publisher Don, who by giving me such a tight deadline, has made me produce something I really like, and possibly put me off writing for life. Paul, Don's fine assistant, for being so speedy and efficient during my long distance calls from London, but most of all for being cheery and sweet. Doug Easton, a spy novelist who now owns the tour and travel-design company Doug Easton Travel. This man first suggested I write a book about fifteen years ago. So you can thank or blame him. The professors and students at Goldsmiths University, for giving me useful feedback on the initial chapters of this book. My psychotherapist who guided me when I had a meltdown months into this project and ended up shaping this book. My clever beautiful friends; Carl Skoggard for his particular edit techniques and his encouragement, Nina Silvert, David and Dori for their crucial input while the layout was being set. Marc for your ongoing, and again crucial input, into my character. Yuk. Fat Tony (you know why). Flora and her family who

AIDEN SHAW

give me so much love and let me use their idyllic home in Devon when writing. Also, Vicky and Joe in New York. In fact, everybody who has given me lovely places to write this book. Pepe. Whoever designs and puts together a new Web site for me. Your name goes here on my next book. My dear friends in NA and AA all over the world, but especially my home groups in Soho London (where've you been all my life?). No mind, I'm glad I've found you now. Cheers.

CONTENTS

San Francisco, 1997

"AIDEN SHAW," SAID A VOICE.

I closed the door to the meeting hall on Fifteenth Street and leaned back against it. This was part weariness, due to lack of sleep. After a two-day splurge of drug "enhanced" sex with god knows who and how many men, the remnants of drugs still lingered in my system. More important, it was to ensure that the door was in fact closed behind me and the weight of my body would keep it that way. Surely, anybody in my position would have done the same thing, seeing all those heated faces.

Again and again I heard my name, the angry tones muffled by the heavy door. "Aiden Shaw. Aiden Shaw."

Curiosity got the better of me. I turned around and opened the door a crack, so nobody would know I was there.

A surprisingly large number of people had gathered for the town meeting. The man standing at the front skimmed his notes as he spoke. He seemed very organized and his jeans looked ironed.

"I'm sure you're all aware of the events of the last few weeks, but I'll replay them to open up the discussion. The portrait of Mr. Shaw is art, not pornography, created by the artists Pierre and Gilles and used for a poster to advertise a gay club night."

The people sitting to either side of the speaker all nodded, with varying degrees of speed and enthusiasm. The man's voice seemed to land more heavily on the word *gay*. Maybe he wanted to put a gay rights or prejudice slant on the debate.

"The said artwork was displayed in the window of the clothes shop All American Boy on Castro, and this is when the first complaints began."

His use of the words *the said* sounded like an attempt at courtroom lingo. I wondered how the complaints were worded. *Shaw's dick is too big, too hard, and too in-your-face?*

A man in the crowd stood up. "But for his cowboy boots and hat, Shaw *is* naked," he said. Ironic, I thought, that a shop used a photo of somebody wearing no clothes to sell clothes. "In addition, he does have a hard-on." The man seemed to have trouble getting the word *hard-on* out of his mouth. "Personally, I did not find this offensive, but I just want to be a voice of reason."

"Thank you," said the speaker at the front, and continued without really addressing the man's comments. "The image was also printed on flyers. Here the press reported of how these got into a children's schoolyard."

"Yeah!" and "No!" the horrified crowd shouted.

I closed the door once more, this time out of exasperation, and let out a heavy sigh. Before anybody could spot me, I darted across the road, turned onto Castro, and walked towards Market Street.

It was all too much, ridiculous in fact. How could they take this so seriously? Their reaction had gone too far from a reality I could relate to. My instinct was to get away, hide, and give myself time to consider what to do. There was a bar on my left called Daddy's. Parting the strips of rubber that kept out the weather and glances from passersby, I entered the dimly lit room.

The early evening crowd appeared to be made up of alcoholics, the frustrated on their way home from work, and anybody high enough to need their company—the ideal scenery for knocking back vodka chased with lager. The barman was a hairy clone with a V-shaped torso, completely stunning if not a bit of a caricature.

An experienced barman knows how to work a tip, and I guessed this one had been doing the job for years. The drink he gave me looked to be about six shots. Little did he know I only wanted to feel jaded, not really *be* it. I took a swig of vodka regardless, feeling masculine and cool and maybe a little self-destructive. It was too much, and made me retch. Attempting to settle my stomach, I took a few big gulps of lager. I still wanted to vomit, but the feeling wasn't intense or urgent. Did I look like a seasoned drinker, like the men to my left and right and all around me?

Pondering this, I drew backwards, away from the bar into the darkness. Feeling beer crates against the back of my thighs, I sat down. Every few minutes, silhouettes of customers moved in front of me, heading to the toilet or escaping outside to the street. My mind swung back to the grotesque spectacle at the meeting hall.

Somebody was walking towards me. "Are you . . . Aiden Shaw?" he said.

No, I thought, at the same time nodding yes.

"Cool! You don't know how many fights you've caused between me and my boyfriend."

"I'm sorry," I said, managing to construct a laugh but hoping my words would end this interaction.

"Don't be sorry. I mean, he's just jealous."

I guessed this meant the speaker fancied me. "That's sweet of you to say."

"Anyway, I'll leave you alone. I just wanted to tell you I'm your biggest fan."

He looked embarrassed. "Shucks!" I said, acting embarrassed myself. "I'm flattered."

"You must get that all the time."

"Enough."

"Anyway, like I said, I'll leave you alone."

He shook my hand and turned to go, then turned back. He scrunched up his nose and said, "It must be kind of weird being you."

"Sometimes," I admitted, taking his statement as a question. Not wanting to be too serious, I followed this with another laugh, wondering how believable it was.

It must have worked, because he responded in kind. His laugh rose in pitch to a whooping sound. Shaking his head, he said, to himself it seemed, "Aiden Shaw." Grinning widely, he slapped his thigh and added, "How cool is that!"

I thought the appropriate response this time was to smile.

He went back to his buddy at the bar. Alone again and feeling the vodka, I stared at the wooden floor.

Who the fuck *was* Aiden Shaw? Some porn star character I'd created. This monster was in no way like Little Fella, my nickname for the inner me, my mum's soft, shy, blushing son, the person I'd grown up with, the one I actually liked. Sometimes it felt as though the lumbering, muscle-bound Brit-With-The-Big-Dick (as some magazine called me) had crushed Little Fella. There had been good reason for my creating him. *Aiden Shaw* was a rebellion against my religious upbringing, when I believed gods existed and that the random one my parents had indoctrinated me with was actually listening and gave a damn about anything, let alone how I behaved. What kind of monstrous institution would encourage such a fantasy in a child's innocent, trusting soul?

Somebody else was heading my way. Panicked, I took another swig of vodka. The figure passed me by, moved through the rubber strips, and left the bar. In a half hour or so, I'd feel more comfortable leaving myself. It would be darker then, and due to the alcohol, I'd be a little more numb.

At the beginning of my "career," one of my clients had told me my dick would be the making of me, adding, "and maybe your ruin." That had been years ago. What a journey it had been since then.

1986
Autumn at Brighton Art School

"Hello," I said, a little wary.

"Oh! Hello," came a man's voice that sounded camp. "Is that Alec or Rod?"

Oh my god! It was about the ad. I didn't know whether to hang up or go through with the call. Despite this, I spoke.

"Rod." I didn't like talking on the phone at the best of times but the fact that it was a punter made me feel a jumble of differing things: wary, anxious, excited.

"I'm calling about your advertisement I found in a pub. What's that place called again? The Bullfrog."

"The *Bulldog*," I said. It was the most boring pub in Brighton.

"Whatever. I'm staying at Paul's Seaside B&B."

"On North Street?" I asked, wanting to appear friendly but very aware of the words I spoke and how deeply I pitched my voice. "I live quite near there," I lied.

"Okay. I'm Ricky," said the man. "I'm here visiting my sister. Just for the weekend."

"Nice," I said, meaning nothing in particular and fiddling nervously with the curled-up telephone cord.

"Actually, it's been quite dull."

I didn't care whether he was having a good time or not, but thought I should say, "I'm sorry." Trying to sound like this wasn't my first-ever rentboy call, I said, "Hopefully that's about to change."

His voice became more playful. "I've never done this before."

Good, I thought, *he won't realize I'm a novice*. "That's okay," I said reassuringly.

"Do you work on the body?"

"Sorry?"

"I mean, do you offer . . . 'sports massage'?"

"Well, I'm not *certified*."

"Um!"

"But I'm very good with my hands." I found myself second-guessing everything I said. Did I sound too corny?

"Good with your hands, hey?"

From the way he spoke, I sensed he was visualizing something about himself and my hands on his body, god only knows where.

"Did you hurt yourself exercising?" I asked.

"Oh, no!" He chuckled. "That's not really my thing. I'm quite a big chap."

"I see."

"Anyway, I was picking up Wilhelmina after her morning walk. That's my dachshund. Won lots of medals, apparently . . ."

His breathing sounded labored. I guessed he was nervous or turned on, but not jerking off.

"And . . . I think I pulled something in my back. I wouldn't mind, but I've got to sit through the theater tonight. Then tomorrow I'm preparing a birthday lunch for my sister and *six* of her friends."

"I'm not promising miracles, but I could probably help release some tension."

"That *is* what I need." The speed and tone of his voice shifted. "How much will this *release* cost me?"

"Well, I could probably sort you out in half an hour, which would cost forty pounds. But it sounds like you need a good going over . . ." As I spoke I also listened to myself, and realized that since picking up the receiver I'd been creating a rentboy persona. It was an act. Little Fella wouldn't be so cocky or cheesy. Rod the rentboy wasn't somebody I'd like to meet, and he definitely wasn't somebody with whom I'd want to be intimate. I might not even want sex with him. Regardless, I kept on. "And to do that properly would take an hour. But that would be sixty pounds."

"Um! I shouldn't really," he said, sounding as though there truly was a juggle between health and cost.

"It's only twenty pounds more for the whole hour," I said. Where did I think I was, in Marrakech's Medina, haggling with a market trader?

"Well, I can't let my sister down." Was he really going to use this to justify seeing a rentboy?

"By the time we're done with you, you'll feel real good." Now I had a cowboy twang.

"*We're?*" He sounded surprised.

"Me and Alec. He's a horny little bugger also."

In reality, Alec (real name Cubus) was more heady than physical. We'd met at ART college, become friends, and were now flatmates. He came with a history of drugs and sex. Regarding the drugs, it seemed he had no real preference and his usage was based on whatever he could get his hands on. With sex it was more about whoever could get their hands on him: farmers in haylofts, bikers at petrol stations, truck drivers when hitching, and married men or teenagers in public toilets, because they had nowhere else to do it. He had a crush on me that I didn't return, but it didn't seem to interfere with our friendship. I felt I was in good company when I was with Cubus, and that I could learn from him. It wasn't that he dazzled when it came to talking, but this didn't seem to get in the way of our communicating. He transmitted on his own unique frequency, but somehow I was able to tune in to his wavelength.

The whole rentboy idea first came about late one night when we were drunk. It still made sense the next day when we were sober. Aside from the obvious financial lure, it was also intrinsically counterculture. This excited the rebellious artist in us, which in turn motivated us to try it. And besides, we were bored with school. Over the next few days the idea evolved and within a week we'd decided to give ourselves rentboy names. Instead of Aiden and Cubus we would be Rod and Alec. My rentboy name was a simple visual association to *iron rod*. Cubus's was taken from the E. M. Forster novel *Maurice*, in which there was a character called Alec Scudder.

"Two?" said Ricky. "Very well! You only live once."

My response was a two-syllable laugh. Then, "So, what time were you thinking of?"

"Well . . . let me plan this properly." He made a series of short, humming noises as he thought through the events of the evening. "Theater at seven-thirty . . ."

Cubus walked into the room, a towel around his waist. I tried to look at his defined, hairless body with a stranger's eye, but I couldn't. His parents were South African, and so he had bobbed to the top in the gene pool. His hair was so thick it had a pelt-like quality. If you looked closely into his hazel eyes, you noticed that they were actually speckled. Still, no matter how hard I tried to see him as a sex object, all I could see was my mate Cubus.

To give him a clue as to what I was doing on the phone, I

poked my cheek with my tongue to simulate a dick in my mouth, and then rubbed my fingers together to infer money. First he looked surprised, then he grinned. He understood.

"Does ten o'clock sound okay?" Ricky asked at the other end of the line.

Showing off to Cubus, I said, "Sounds great! And you're happy with sixty pounds for the hour?" Cubus put his hands over his mouth in shock. "So, Paul's Seaside B&B, ten o'clock . . . Out front's fine . . . I look forward to it, too. See you then."

I put the receiver down.

"Oh my god!" said Cubus. "Sixty fucking pounds!"

I put my hands behind my head. "Hey! Nobody mentioned *fucking*."

"Legally, are you even allowed to say that on the phone?"

"I don't know," I said. "And I don't care. We're going to be rich. *Sixty* pounds! Fuck off overdraft! Fuck off poverty!"

"Fuck everybody," said Cubus. "If they'll pay us."

After a moment of childlike excitement, I dropped into a more serious tone.

"You know what? I don't know if I was more worried that somebody *would* call, or . . ."

Cubus anticipated what I was going to say. "That *nobody* would call!" we said at the same time.

"Ever," I added dramatically, but meaning it.

After three days of putting up ads, our initial enthusiasm had begun to mix with uncertainty, if not embarrassment.

"Why did we think anybody would call? It was hardly sophisticated marketing."

"I don't know," said Cubus, a little defensive. "Using the college photocopier to print the cards was clever."

"Sure, and putting them up in gay pubs was cheeky."

"Don't knock it. We got a call, didn't we?"

I laughed. "You've got to give me some credit, too. It was my idea to put them in public phone boxes. That was good, wasn't it?"

"*Good*, I don't know. *Outrageous*, definitely."

Heaving a sigh of relief, I said, "All that worrying for nothing. When it came to it, talking to him, it just all came out. Like I was a natural. You should have heard me."

Cubus slipped on underwear as he spoke. "Why didn't you call me?"

"There wasn't time. He kept talking. But I think I pulled it off."

"Sure sounded like it." He made a whooping noise. "Get us!"

We continued talking as we got ready—excited, not stopping, shouting down the hall from different rooms. Slightly hyper, I ran out to pick up some lager and, knowing we could afford it now, also bought vodka. The more we drank, trying to relax, the more excited we became. Once dressed and ready, we sat in the kitchen and didn't even attempt to contain ourselves. As far as we knew how, we were both in rentboy drag (as opposed to looking like the art students we actually were). To anybody else the difference probably wouldn't have been noticeable. Unable to sit still a moment longer, we had no choice but to set off.

We arrived early at Paul's Seaside B&B, at nine forty-five, and hung around outside acting as though we were just friends chatting, but feeling very illegal. I thought that if I *felt* like a rentboy it was more likely that Ricky would believe I *was* one. So in my head I kept repeating, *Rentboy rentboy rentboy*, in the hope that this would somehow work through my body, seep through my pores, and coat me, serving as both disguise and armor.

At quarter past ten, just enough time for me to start feeling demoralized because Ricky hadn't shown up, he appeared at the doorway. Didn't he have a clock in his room?

"Rod? Alec?" he said in a loud voice meant to be a whisper.

"That's right," I said.

"Come in."

Cubus and I followed him inside and up two flights of stairs. Ricky said nothing. Being in front of Cubus, I had to watch Ricky's huge bum bobbing around too close to my face. A bum smell trailed behind him, but not the kind I liked. At the door to his room he paused, sighed, opened it a little, and edged in as though there was something behind it. Suspicious, if not a bit scared. I wondered if there was somebody waiting to jump us—a thug or, worse, the police. On my guard, I followed Ricky tentatively into his room, surprised, relieved, and quite confused to find only his dog, on a special little velvet cushion.

Ricky sat on the bed as though it was a throne. "Well, well, well, Wilhelmina," he said, picking up his dog and holding her in front of his face. "What do we have here?" he said, adding, "What lovely young things they are," to make sure she was focusing properly.

The way he spoke reminded me of the Wicked Witch of the West in *The Wizard of Oz*. *Mad bitch*, I thought—Ricky, not Wilhelmina—*and himself so far from being a lovely thing*.

"What do we think of them, Willy?"

Oh, no. A sausage dog called Willy.

While Willy decided, I took note of Ricky's appearance. He was unusually pear-shaped, with a hairline so high it made his hair look perched, and considering the room wasn't even hot, he was sweating too much for it to be healthy. It looked as though his intention was to wear dress clothes. His shirt was buttoned all the way up to the collar and he wore a bow tie, which I supposed he referred to as his dickey-bow. His trousers might have passed as smart in the dim lighting of a theater, but in the cruel light of Paul's Seaside B&B it was clear that the fabric was stay-press. He was covered with Willy hair that was especially dense on his lap and made it look like his crotch area was hairy. Although Ricky's visuals detracted from his sex appeal, I held out hope. Maybe his attitude would surprise me.

It did, but not because it turned me on.

"Now, let's see these young bodies. Strip!"

It seemed fair to assume that Ricky's first sentence addressed his dog. The second, spoken more as a command, he directed at Cubus and me. We looked at each other at virtually the same moment. Unless I was mistaken, Cubus was as confused, amused, and scared as I was. At least we had each other for support. The trouble was, for me it felt more embarrassing with Cubus there. Alone, I could handle being degraded. To make things worse, there had been no lead-in, no slow seduction, no time for us to conjure up any feelings of sexiness or being aroused.

Cubus pulled me a smile which I read as *We've come this far, we may as well . . .*

Our T-shirts were the first to go. Not knowing what to do with it, I followed Cubus's lead and tucked it through one of my belt loops. With pantomime theatricality, Ricky licked his lips.

"Um, lovely! Boy flesh."

"Cheers," I said, which probably sounded random, but I was trying to keep myself part of his fantasy.

Ricky overlooked the fact that I'd spoken. "Now the pants."

Pants. Why couldn't he have said *jeans*? Was he purposely trying to emasculate me, infantilize me? Again I looked to Cubus for some indication of how to respond. He was already pushing his jeans around his ankles. Unbuttoning my jeans, I pulled them down over my thighs, but let them rest on my knees.

Ricky spoke directly to me. "All the way down. Naughty boy."

I pushed my jeans down completely and stood up straight, but felt particularly exposed, presumably because Cubus was there. This was odd, because we saw each other in underpants all

SORDID TRUTHS

the time at home, even in front of pickups. But it felt very different in front of a punter. It was as if Cubus acted as a mirror and on some level I didn't like seeing myself doing what Ricky ordered, and felt something like shame.

"Ooo! Meaty boy thighs." Ricky's face was a jumble of Mad Scientist and Evil Ruler of the Universe. For a second, I felt admired, almost sexy, but then he ruined it by adding, "Look, Wilhelmina!" The fact that he'd used the dog's full name somehow made it worse.

Not wanting to be there anymore, especially not standing in my underpants, I nudged my crotch self-consciously. Despite Ricky's madness and Cubus's presence, another thing running through my head was, if Ricky asked me to get naked, would my dick look okay. As a diversion I said, "Do you like a gentle massage or a firm one?"

For my insolence he looked me sternly in the eye and said, "We'll get to that . . ." With a whimsical inflection he added, "Maybe."

In response, Cubus let out a single gust of laughter. It took me by surprise. With Diva Ricky headlining, Cubus was beginning to merge into the background for me. Cubus's response must have been nerves, because nothing funny had happened. Well, not *ha-ha* funny. I turned towards him.

Ricky instantly directed my attention back to himself. "And the rest," he said, not realizing his acting was so hammy. Then, to his dog, "Off with their knickers!"

Was he for real? Now he'd changed roles and was hashing another character, that of a Roman Emperor wielding his power over someone's life, or in this case my dignity.

Everything changed the instant I slid down my underpants and my dick plopped out. I thought it comical, the way it bounced slightly, as though it knew it was being funny.

"Oh, lord!" Ricky said, lunging forward on his knees before it came to a standstill.

The next thing I knew, he had his mouth on my dick, with his palms around the sides of it as though he was praying. As he did this, he adopted yet another character. While managing to maintain his weirdly pear-shaped and unintentionally dressed-up appearance, he transformed into a groveling submissive. My startled response was to back off, but fortunately this only happened in my head. I barely flinched. It didn't matter. In his current state of emergency Ricky wouldn't have noticed. More importantly, he wouldn't have cared. Whatever my reaction, ultimately this wasn't about me.

In stunned silence, I turned to Cubus. He looked more shocked than I felt. This was understandable, because he had a better view of the proceedings. Whereas I *was* the proceedings. So when Ricky said, "Please sir! Please sir! Please can I suck your massive boy meat?" Cubus had to cover his mouth with both hands to stifle his laughter.

Meanwhile I couldn't help thinking, surely massive *man* meat had a better ring to it. But Ricky was the one paying, so he could alliterate as badly as he wanted. I could only guess that youth was a big part of his fantasy, and sucking a boy must feel more exciting than sucking a twenty-year-old who considered himself fully adult. At this moment all I knew for certain—and somewhat to my surprise—was that my dick was hard. It stood straight up, solid against my tummy. In the wrong context, having too hard a dick can be a problem. It wasn't sitting at a good angle for Ricky to get it into his mouth with conviction. All he could do was bob at the end, looking like a rabbit gnawing on a carrot. Then ingeniously, he stood up, bent over, and went at it more competently.

Cubus was looking my way. I shrugged to him, referring to

Ricky and meaning, *whatever makes the punter happy*. Ricky's technique brought my attention back to my crotch. He was quite the expert dick sucker. His enthusiasm and work ethic on such a task made me realize it was true: Being sucked felt good. It didn't matter who did it. With Ricky wholeheartedly occupied, I was free to ponder the situation.

Fact: Having my dick sucked wasn't a bad way to pass time.

Fact: I liked orgasms.

Fact: From now on, I could be paid for physical pleasure.

Fact: The whole process was bound to leave me satisfied, and there'd be no need to trouble myself for an orgasm again for at least a few hours, maybe even until tomorrow.

Fact: Pubs, clubs, and the cruising area on the four-mile strip from the West Pier to the Bushes along the sea front would probably lose some of their magic lure for me.

Fact: Money would no longer be a worry.

Conclusion: Being a rentboy was without a doubt a sensible job—if I wanted to be fancy, perhaps even a noble one. How else would a man like Ricky ever have the chance to suck anybody's dick? Surely nobody would knowingly allow him to. I felt a surge of goodwill. Within a short time, this feeling morphed and dropped down my body into a more genital, excited sensation.

"I'm close to cumming," I warned.

Although I directed this statement at Ricky, it was actually to give Cubus the heads-up. While keeping in character of somebody having the most amazing blowjob ever, I looked at Cubus. He had his arms folded and was miming tapping his foot. I smiled at him. He blew a silent sigh out of the corner of his mouth, pretended to look at his watch, and made a round-it-up action with his hands, the way they did on film sets. Ricky had not even touched Cubus. Clearly the deciding factor must have been my dick. Cubus had a much better body and was more beautiful, but his dick, although as thick, was not as long as mine.

The suck-monster continued to slurp, but now it was as though his life depended on it. His whole body writhed and went into spasm. *Jesus!* Something cold dribbled out of his dick.

"Sorry." He stopped for a moment to explain. "It happens to Wilhelmina also."

Oh my god! He was referring to piss. I'd read somewhere that little dogs had a tendency to do it when excited. But why was it cold? Alarmed and annoyed, I wished that I hadn't taken my boots off, because some of his piss landed on one of my socks.

The dog must have liked the look of what was going on. That, or she smelled sex or piss, some delicious scent. It's possible she used whatever heightened sense of surroundings dogs possess, because now she darted manically between our legs in what appeared to be a complex routine. Sometimes she'd make a figure eight around my feet, and then she did the same to Ricky. Just when I thought I'd figured her out, she'd loop both of us as though rounding up cattle.

In the face of all the distractions that fought for top billing in this freak show, somehow I began to cum. Cautiously, I said, "I'm cumming." Being new at this, I didn't know what was allowed.

"Cum! Cum! Cum!" urged Ricky, sucking faster and even better.

"I'm cumming!"

For a perfect moment, life paused and enhanced. Joy consumed my entire body. Into this bliss came a scratchy, ferret-like voice: "I'm cumming, too."

Post-orgasm, a different sensation tore me back to Paul's Seaside B&B, that of my now hypersensitive dick still being sucked. Fortunately it wasn't long before Ricky slowed, then stopped. I looked down at him and affectionately rubbed the top of his head. He pulled away, seemingly annoyed.

"Retarded little bitch!" he said.

I followed his eyes to the dog, who was attempting to lick his cum, which had landed on her face. But her snail-like tongue couldn't reach past her thin lips and tiny tombstone teeth. It looked comical. It also turned my stomach. I wondered if I'd have felt differently if it wasn't Ricky's cum but somebody's I fancied— or if it wasn't Wilhelmina. This thought made me shudder. It was all getting too bestial for my taste.

Ricky jumped up and busied himself with moving things around. Quite roughly, he picked up his dog, dropped her in the en suite bathroom, and slammed the door shut. When he returned, Cubus and I were getting dressed. My mind was on how the exchange of money would work.

We waited and waited. Finally Ricky said, "Haven't you two got homes to go to?"

Once again he'd managed to shock me. His nonlinear, pin-ball-like mind was impossible to follow, let alone anticipate.

Boldly, Cubus said, "We're waiting for . . ."

"Spit it out," said Ricky.

"The money."

"Oh, yeah. Just a sec and I'll walk you downstairs." This *sec* consisted of his rummaging around in his suitcase, straightening his bow tie, and flattening his hair with his hands. *Now* he cared about looking decent.

To fill in the time, I said, "What did you see at the theater?"

Without looking up from his suitcase, he said, "It's a new play, you probably won't have heard of it."

"Try me."

My comment made him stand up, but instead of facing me he looked straight ahead. His focus must have been the corner of a wardrobe. "It's called *Prick Up Your Ears*," he said impatiently.

Cubus let out an "Ah!" I understood this as acknowledgment.

To my surprise, and a little to my disappointment, my feelings towards Ricky changed. I'd been thinking him a complete wacko. Hearing him mention something that I could relate to took away his otherness. Suddenly I felt embarrassed for being so judgmental.

"I'm familiar with Orton," I said in the most natural voice I'd used since first speaking to Ricky on the phone.

Now back in his suitcase, he responded sarcastically, "I expect you'll be seeing it then."

"I saw it last week."

He twisted his neck up to face me, looking his most grotesque yet. "Oh, really!" he said, and smirked as though he'd caught me out. "Tonight was opening night."

"We went to the dress rehearsal," Cubus chirped in. "Our friend plays Halliwell."

Ricky screwed up his face so tight, it looked like it might disappear into itself.

"Who?"

This was Cubus's problem now. "Kenneth Halliwell. The one who killed Joe."

"Oh, yeah. Depressing, wasn't it."

Under the misguided belief that we might manage a real conversation, I said, "I thought it had a certain feel-good quality to it, in a weird kind of way."

Ricky stood up and looked to his side dramatically in a mirror he must have known was there. Like Joan Crawford or some other old Hollywood legend, he rolled his eyes and said, exasperated, "I assumed there'd be more sex in it."

"It's all about sex, really," I offered. "Although I admit they don't show much. It's more implied."

Ricky seemed more concerned with whether the tuft of hair on his forehead should slant to the left or the right. With a surprising amount of anger, he said to his reflection, "There could have been *some*."

Sensing I should back off, I said, "I guess so." Then, after a moment of silence, "Still, it must have shocked your sister?"

With a loud tut-tut, he said, "*She* didn't go!" and spun about with surprising agility. "Okay. Out of here! But *you* . . ." he said, poking me. "You should be in movies." Then he laughed, clearly *at* me. "*Porn*, I mean. I have contacts. Maybe we could . . ." He circled his forefinger on my chest, like a woman in a 1970s film seducing a younger man. "If you know what I mean." The last word came out more as a purr than an actual word, nothing like a cat but a lot like a provincial drag queen.

"That's kind of you," I lied. "I'm flattered," I continued, still lying, "but I don't think it would be good for my future career, whatever that might be."

"Listen, honey, you have the dick of death. Or the font of all *life*." He laughed at his own incredible wit. "It'll be the making of you. Mark my words. Then again, it may be your ruin." He sounded like a gypsy cursing me. He should have ended his statement with a theatrically evil *ha ha haaa*!

With a light grip on my left biceps, Ricky guided me (and therefore Cubus) out of the room and hurried us down the stairs. He took us to the entrance of the B&B, and once we were outside, he spoke loudly, with part of his body behind the door. "Tell your Aunty I'll call her later." Winking conspiratorially, he passed me an envelope. "And don't forget to give her this birthday card."

Cubus and I burst out laughing. Was there no end to his madness? Who was he trying to fool? There was nobody around.

Evidently that was the last straw. Ricky closed the door firmly, without saying another word.

We were happy to get away from him, but what concerned us more was that we wanted to look in the envelope. Once off

North Street we huddled in the doorway of a closed shop. Cubus pulled the envelope out of my hands and tore it open. We looked on in wonder, as if we'd discovered a newborn alien baby. Inside a thank-you card with a rabbit on it, there was not just the sixty pounds we'd asked for, but a whole twenty-pound note extra.

Summer 1989
The Burlington

Saturday

"SHUSH!" I WHISPERED. "BE QUIET."

"Why?" Terry mouthed.

I cupped my hand to my ear and simultaneously put a finger against my lips. Outside the cubicle there were nightclub toilet sounds: murmurs of voices in the queue waiting, shuffling feet, trickling water, and the deep bass from the dance floor, which I could also *feel*.

"Sorry, baby," I said quietly. "I thought I heard security."

"Well hurry up and do your coke then," said Terry.

I crouched down and did my line off the toilet seat. I started to unroll the ten-pound note.

"Hey! That's mine, remember."

"No way!" I said. "I bet you get away with that sometimes."

I poked him affectionately in the ribs. We had no shirts on, because we were already high, and trying to cool down while also showing off our bodies. After three months of sex with Terry, I still wasn't bored. This was very unusual for me. It might have had something to do with the fact that he had soft, sticking-up, caramel-color hair, and even softer pale skin, or possibly, it was his little red nose that looked as though he'd been kissing for hours. Equally, it could have been the milky smell his skin gave off, even in smoky nightclubs. The most endearing thing of all about Terry was his sleepy eyes, day or night, that made him look newborn. These things together made me want to take care of him, and fuck him too.

He flicked open the top button of his jeans. "Security," he said, pulling his bottom lip under his front teeth. "Does that mean I'm safe?"

I shook my head. "No fucking way, mate."

"Oh, no!" he said melodramatically.

"Is that a dare?" I said, hoping.

"Dunno."

I pressed against him, pinning him to the cubicle wall, my tongue going deep into his mouth to show I wanted to be inside him. After a couple of minutes I pulled my head back.

"Damn," I said. "You're so *on* tonight."

"On *you*, if I'm lucky."

There was a knock on the door. "Sorry, mate," I said to the person outside. "One minute . . ." I paused. " . . . Bad stomach!" Terry covered his mouth to keep from laughing. " . . . Think it's the pills!"

"No problem," came a voice with nightclub sincerity. Most people waiting knew the cubicles were primarily for drugs, sex, and the shits caused by ecstasy. Initially Terry and I had only gone in to do a quick line, but he was so irresistible.

In an attempt to keep the volume of my voice low, I spoke directly into Terry's ear, aware that it was breathy and hot. "Did I say please?"

"You must have," he whispered, his eyes widening, "because you have backstage access. Actually all areas. VIP."

"You mean that?"

Terry leaned into me and rested his head on my chest. "It's

very likely the drugs talking, and I'm sure I'll really regret it in the morning, but . . . yes."

I turned his face towards mine. "Funny man!" I said. "You think I'll be done with you by morning?" Raising my eyebrows, I continued, "If so, think again." Not everybody made me speak in such a corny way, but Terry drew it out of me. I twisted my head down and around so that his face was only an inch from mine. "Terry," I said solemnly," I love you . . ." I paused. " . . . From the bottom of my *E*."

He pulled away from me, rolling his eyes, and we both burst out laughing. Immediately there was a knock.

"Eh! Come on, mate," said the same voice as before. "Don't take the piss."

"Sorry," I replied. "One minute."

Terry whispered to me. "You're too much!"

"Better too much than not enough, eh?"

"Too much of you"—Terry wriggled his thin hips—"is just enough."

I pulled him gently towards me again. "A word of advice from someone older and wiser. *Too Much* is just getting going."

"You're such a fool," he said, his lips now on mine so I could feel the words.

In an old Hollywood crooner voice I said, "You gotta love me, though."

"I've *gotta*, have I? Gee!" he said with a dumb cartoon smile. "Well . . . okay."

"So, it's a date." I undid the latch of the toilet door. Before opening it I said, "This place closes in about an hour, then you're mine. Right!"

Outside, a line of other shirtless men waited, dazed. They chewed their cheeks as though they all had gum in their mouths. Some seemed indignant, possibly put out by the wait. Others looked as though they'd forgotten why they were there. One person stood out from the rest. He appeared to be in a pool of soft, fuzzy light, so out of place in the piss rank toilets of Heaven. (My E must have had quite a lot of acid in it.)

It was David.

I'd seen him around London several times over the last few months. To me it meant nothing to sleep around and not care. My attitude towards most men was blasé. But with this David chap it was different. I didn't dare to even try and pick him up. And somehow I felt that coming out of a cubicle with a sexy lad like Terry needed explaining. In the hope of masking my embarrassment, I affected a "home boy" persona and nudged one of my nostrils with my thumb, to indicate that Terry and I had been snorting coke. David smiled—something not many did in clubs—and, most unusual of all, it looked genuine.

Oblivious to my thoughts, Terry went out of the toilet, leaving me with David. I leaned towards him slightly and said, "I . . ." but stopped, looking from side to side to check that nobody else could hear. "I think . . ." Again I didn't finish my sentence. This was probably because I meant what I was saying. Finally I managed, "I think you're beautiful."

David smiled again. "Thanks." Somebody shuffled between us to get to a urinal, and at the same time a cubicle became free. David headed towards it, turned, and said, "Nice seeing you again." As the door closed, I felt I was in the final scene of some *film noir* with the camera slowly pulling away, taken out of my high. But I didn't mind, because David had caused it.

I took a quick look in the mirror and went back into the strobing, smoky, humid heat of the club. My high returned. Terry must have gone back to his mates upstairs, but we'd be sure to see each other when the lights came on as the club closed. Reassured, I headed onto the dance floor, to where I'd left Cubus. He was easy to spot, because the gel in his hair glowed in the fluorescent light.

Heaven was much the same as it had been ten years earlier, when I was thirteen and it was *the* nightclub. I'd felt small-town compared to the big city Punks, Goths, and New Romantics that frequented it. Since then the entire club scene had declined, but now it had been resurrected. This wasn't because of groundbreaking DJs, state-of-the-art lighting, intriguing interiors, or fabulous club kids, but because of a drug called ecstasy. All the papers wrote of the euphoria, hallucinatory effects, and feelings of empathy produced by E. Personally, I found it depended on the individual pill. On a weak E, I felt pleasant and slightly flushed; on a strong one, I loved everything and sweated a lot.

Cubus and I danced until the track jarred with our high. I made a "Fancy a drink?" sign with one hand. He nodded, and we headed off the dance floor towards the nearest bar, pulling up to it like a couple of cowboys and ordering two bottles of water. Even though shirtless, with our jeans, footwear, and hair we were attempting *looks*. Cubus was doing rentboy-off-duty drag, as he called it (I referred to it as catalog-model). With a fit body and a face that morphed between Disney cute and deeply troubled depending on the thought in his head at the time, he looked his age, early twenties. I was aiming for a fresh-from-the-gym look—incongruous when drug-fucked in a nightclub but quite the trend.

"Cute crowd," said Cubus.

"Yeah," I replied. "Good E."

Cubus leaned forward, folded his arms, and rested them on the bar, his pert bum at a forty-five-degree angle. He blew air out of his cheeks and sighed deeply, clearly rushing. On a strong pill most people sat down; some even puked, especially first-timers.

"You all right?" I said.

"Yeah." He paused. "Great music."

I squinted. "Like I said, *good E.*"

Cubus looked confused until the sounds coming from my mouth made sense. Due to the E his body language showed relaxation, yet his face, moving of its own accord, was approaching the look of a mass of worms. Still he managed to shape its chaos into a smile of comprehension. I envied the intensity of his high, and decided to deal with my feelings in a mature, insightful, proactive way.

"Cubus," I said, popping another pill. "I'll be right with you."

"Whoa!" said Cubus, feeling another rush.

"Strong, huh? Jesus!"

"No *Jesus* here," he said, pausing to cope with his high. "Just one very fucked-up Mary."

"How do you manage to make jokes when so high?"

Half leaning, he put his arms around me and said, "I love you."

Now I felt like the character Bert in *Sesame Street*. "Duh!" I said. "I love you too, Ernie."

This was actually true. More importantly, it *felt* true. The pills were working; we hadn't wasted our money. Over Cubus's shoulder, I saw Terry standing by himself, just a few feet away, awkwardly playing with his fingers like a little boy. Continuing to hug Cubus, I called Terry over for a classic group-E hug.

"Cubus, are you staying at Kyle's place or ours?" I asked, knowing the answer.

"Kyle's away. I don't really want to go back to an empty flat when I'm this fucked up."

To some degree I regretted what I said next, as it meant I'd be forfeiting the sexually depraved night I wanted with Terry, but I hoped that at some point we might still get at least a few hours alone in bed.

"Well, here's *a* plan. It's not necessarily *the* plan. We could get some more pills, go back to our flat, and get really fucked up."

"Can't argue with such reasonable logic," said Terry.

"Isn't my room full of cobwebs by now?" said Cubus.

My guess was that Cubus's comment was less about physical comfort than about spending time with me under the same roof. He hadn't been staying at Kyle's because he liked him so much. The passing years had not changed Cubus's romantic feelings towards me, and my lack of response in kind was finally putting a strain on our relationship. So Cubus took every opportunity that offered itself to stay away from me. Kyle was just one of a stable of shags. Admittedly he did heroin, an old favorite of Cubus's, and apparently this gave them a great deal in common.

"You won't notice the cobwebs when so high," I said, and added, "The bugs may even talk to you." Cubus liked to trip, so I thought this notion might appeal to him.

Terry grinned at me like a child on Christmas morning. God love him! He was so easy to please.

"First things first." I said. "That E I just necked was our last."

Without hesitation Cubus and I each pulled out fat wads of cash.

I jumped in with, "Let me use mine. I'm still trying to get rid of the money that New Yorker gave me.

"Okay. That did seem like an easy gig."

Who spent what money didn't concern us. We both had too much of it, and there always seemed to be so much more coming our way.

"If I buy twenty then I'll probably get a deal," I said. The going rate was twenty-five pounds, but they were usually cheaper in bulk.

I scanned the room. Nothing. Then I remembered that the best place to look was the dimly lit arches that led to the dance floor. It was a good place to take somebody for a little privacy if you fancied a grope. In addition, it was a good area to do anything illicit, illegal, or ill-thought-out. I focused in that direction. Even in the half-light of that little microcosm of a world, I could have sworn that the drug dealer I recognized was looking at me. Maybe he had a sixth sense.

"I've spotted somebody," I said. "I'll just prepare the cash."

It was always best to have the correct amount ready before approaching a dealer. With my body angled towards the bar I counted out money, splitting three hundred pounds into four fifty-pound notes, four twenties, and two tens. That way, if the dealer wanted to give me a discount I'd still have the right amount ready.

Finally, I said, "Sorted, kids," and hid the cash between my palm and a Coke can I'd picked up off the bar. Before I left, I said, as casually as possible, "Cubus, see if there's anybody here you want to drag home, in case you're horny later."

As odd as it seems, I believed the dealer's eyes were still on me, while at the same time, like the Hindu god Kali his arms and hands seemed to multitask about him—waving hello, giving high fives, patting people on their backs, accepting drinks and cigarettes. For a moment this mesmerized me. Now he seemed like Medusa from Greek mythology. Perhaps it was the flashing and changing lighting that gave the illusion of movement, but his wild, naturally curly shoulder-length hair looked alive, going anywhere it pleased. The visual was slightly unsettling, even a bit scary. I reminded myself that the E I'd taken was trippy. He probably wasn't a monster but just a dealer with long, curly hair. With him still looking directly at me, at least it would be easy to get his attention. Unless he was blind, and that was his only sight line. Regardless, I was on a mission and this creature had what I needed.

Now near enough to speak, I leaned towards him. With a gesture of his hands, he made everybody around him disappear into the darkness. What power.

"Hey," I said. "Got any pills?"

"No," he said. His eyes, still fixed on mine, followed me as I moved, so there was nothing wrong with his sight. But despite their intensity, they showed no emotion.

"No problem." I turned to go, feeling a bit weird.

"But I can sort you out," he said. "Ask that blond in the shorts, over by the cigarette machine." He pointed to a skinny boy who looked to be about fifteen.

"He's a dealer?" I asked, surprised.

"Well, just between you and me, he works for me."

"Works for you . . . ?"

I couldn't make out this Medusa Man. Something about him—rather, *many* things about him—didn't gel. His eyes had the shiny, fixed quality of stuffed animals. The rest of his face didn't move much either, except for a small area around his mouth that only seemed capable of slanting up at one side.

"My name's Trev," he said. Before I could tell him my name, he added, "And you're Aiden."

"Have we met?"

Suddenly he was bashful, simple-looking. "I just know who you are."

"Hello, Trev."

I stepped in to shake his hand. Up close his skin seemed much older than it should be. It didn't correspond with his persona, voice, clothes, or demeanor.

"I've seen you around and just wanted to meet you," he said diffidently, as though he knew exactly how I felt looking at him.

"Cheers, I think."

"How many did you want?"

"Twenty."

"That's big money. Oh, yeah, of course. You're a Burlington boy. Go tell that blond what you want, and tell him to look over here."

Something weird was going on, but I guessed it was in my favor. I approached the boy. As requested, he looked to Trev, who did something with his hand on the back of his neck. Then the kid looked at me a moment too long, as though we were in love or he was going to knife me, something beautiful in a Jean Genet kind of way. He nodded at his mate behind me, who put his arm over my shoulder.

"Here, pal," he said, and led me away as though we were old friends. "We're going to have a little walk and I'm going to put something in your right pocket."

If he weren't beautiful and smiling, I would have been scared. "Okay," I said, game for most things when high.

We stopped. He kissed me, quite realistically, said, "So call me," and left.

I put my hand in my pocket and found a big plastic bag full of what felt like pills, but I didn't dare pull them out in the club.

I went straight back to Cubus and Terry. With perhaps too much secrecy and paranoia, I told them that I wanted to get out of the club as quickly as possible. Cubus nodded at a short, sleazy-looking Spaniard who introduced himself as Javier while we made our way towards the exit. The music stopped and the lights came on. As we approached the arch where I'd met Trev, I thought to stop and say thank you, but Trev and all his cronies had vanished.

Monday

I SAT UP IN BED AND LOOKED AT THE WALL IN FRONT of me. I'd painted it dark blue and rubbed metallic powder into it, which gave it an iridescent sheen that reminded me of a butterfly's wing. In the center of this wall was a cross I'd made out of twigs and thorny red roses. Despite my rebelling against Catholicism, I loved the iconography and the passionate, sometimes brutal imagery. Out of the corner of my eye I saw the digital clock at the head of my bed flip on to 1-2-0-0. *Make a wish*, I thought, trying to remember who'd first made me aware of this idea. The large red numbers glowed dangerously, warning that time was passing or running out, or maybe just that it was time to do something else. I sighed and rolled onto my tummy. The thin cotton gauze over the window made the air in the room appear as though it held memories, almost audible. It was how I imagined the inside of a pharaoh's tomb would look, feel, and sound. Maybe I'd taken too much acid over the last few years.

"Come on," I said quietly, then stood up, wondering how my voice sounded as I walked out of my bedroom. The four-inch multicolor dots slipped by on the hallway wall. A month ago I'd felt they validated me. Now they lacked authenticity. Presumably the walls had once been white, but by the time I moved in they were grubby. To make them cleaner and more my own, I'd painted them primary red. When this became shabby, I revived it with lime green. In turn, for no reason other than that I had the time and money, I replaced this with wasp-like black and yellow stripes.

In my kitchen I was confronted by Christmas. The walls were covered with wrapping paper, and seasonal baubles hung from the top of the window frame. (After the twenty-fifth of December, holiday things are very cheap to buy.) I liked to think that it looked like a Christmas present turned inside out—which meant the world outside the room was a gift and I was reality. Christo-capitalism was deeply embedded in my consciousness, my mind stagnant with retained knowledge and childhood disappointments. Several times each day, my kitchen managed to surprise me, which showed me that my thoughts and feelings hadn't yet evolved. With great patience I waited to become numb, if only to the imagery. But I'd had it the same for over a year and my Ghosts of Christmas Past still haunted me.

The sink was packed with dirty dishes. To fill the kettle I had to edge a cup between gray water and the cold tap, then empty it into the kettle. After doing this three times I switched the kettle on and went into the living room.

The four walls, ceiling, and floor were all painted matte gray, giving it a solid, castle-like feel. The only furniture was a black futon, a low coffee table also painted gray, and a TV, all adding to the room's lack of coziness. I stood by the window, ignoring the amazing view of Parliament and the Thames, looking instead at the dirt on the glass. It wasn't going to go away, so I changed my focus. This was how I dealt with things sometimes. From the dirt inches from my eyes, my focus traveled to a bunch of tatty and grubby pigeons that looked as though they could have been flying in a smoggy London sky a hundred years ago. Then my sight advanced to the nearest tower blocks, their windows offering glimpses into other people's lives. In the block nearest to mine a thickset bald man stood in a brown dressing gown. He was facing my way and held a cup in his hand. It appeared he was looking at me, so I lifted my hand and waved. He did the same.

I heard the kettle switch off, and headed back to make a cup of coffee. I looked in the fridge for milk but the only things I found were old butter, half a jar of pickles, a bottle of poppers, and some acidophilus capsules, all useful at the right time but not when I wanted coffee. I couldn't be bothered to go down to the shop. Worse still, I couldn't think of any reason why I shouldn't wash the dishes. So I emptied the cold gray water from the sink and filled it with hot, squirting washing liquid into the jet of the taps. Once it was full I stood motionless, simply enjoying the comfort of having my hands in the heat of the soapy water. My thoughts fell back to Sunday morning.

Terry, Cubus, Javier, and I got home sometime after three. The first thing we did was to look at the drug stash. It seemed best to put the ecstasy into a bowl of some sort—a dark one, so we could easily see the pills. A blue papier-mâché fruit bowl seemed ideal. I wiped this out with my handkerchief and placed it on the coffee table in the living room.

As though looking at something holy, we all crouched around the table, exclaiming, "Fuck!" "God!" "Shit!" "Ah!" as the E poured and settled into the bowl.

"How many did you ask for?" said Cubus.

"Twenty."

"That's not twenty," said Terry, shaking his head, his mouth open.

I put my arms around him and nuzzled his neck from behind.

"Why don't you count them, baby, and tell us how many we've got to get through."

"Okay," he said, and sat cross-legged, counting them into four piles as the rest of us looked on. "Twenty-nine . . . ," he said.

"Thirty!" finished Cubus. "Holy fuck!"

"This is normal?" Javier asked.

"No!" Cubus and I said.

Terry just carried on, grinning. I think he was used to getting things for free.

"What the fuck will you have to do for these?" said Cubus.

"Nobody said anything about *strings*," I responded.

"People don't just throw this kind of money around for nothing. He's up to something. He probably wants *you* up *him*."

Cubus had every right to be suspicious, but not to let it ruin our fun. I'd already been through how weird it all was, and thought of it as past tense now.

"We'll deal with that when it comes," I said. "For now, let's party on. Drink, anybody?"

Nods and yes noises ensued.

"Vodka's all we got, I'm afraid, with Diet Coke and OJ. Oh, and one can of cider, if you count that."

Javier came with me to help. I gave him glasses and a bottle of vodka. To save getting up again, we brought everything to the living room at once. When I walked out from the kitchen, I saw Cubus looking into my bedroom, a weird expression on his face. It surprised me that he wasn't looking in his own room, and so I watched him. Several seconds passed.

"Oh!" he said as he turned back towards me.

I remained quiet, wondering how he'd explain himself.

At first he didn't. Then he came towards me, saying, "I just wondered if you'd been decorating."

"Not since you were last here."

"Drink. Good." He headed past me, into the living room.

After a few drinks Cubus grabbed a handful of E's and left. Javier's place was just around the corner.

Terry and I partied until Sunday afternoon. At some point we took sleeping tablets. It was bliss as I held him from behind. Being exhausted and on sleepers, we slept until Monday. He'd only left about an hour ago.

I switched on the TV in the living room, to the news. There had been some horrible massacre in China, a place called Tiananmen Square. Ugh! No wonder I took ecstasy.

The doorbell rang. Shit. I dried my hands quickly, popped into the bathroom, glanced in the mirror and stroked my hair flat, pulled a glob of sleep out of the corner of my eye, and went to answer the door.

"Hey, Bill! Nice to see you," I lied.

He looked at his watch.

"I didn't see the time," I lied again. "I ended up having a bit of a late night."

He just stood there, leaning forward slightly. He was dressed heavily for such a warm day. He had on a shirt that looked two sizes too small, with a tie so tight it made his face red. His jacket looked to be made of wool, or something like it. He was obviously feeling the heat, because beads of sweat covered the shiny skin on the top of his head, and his collar was wet.

"Come in," I said. "Take your jacket off. You must be boiling."

Bill was one of my regulars. The upside to this arrangement was that there were no weird surprises, and money I could rely on. The downside was boredom and the fact that I gave Bill a discount. It was normal to give regulars a bargain rate, but because the sex was always predictable I felt they should pay more. Uncertainty was one of the things that attracted me to prostitution, and weird surprises definitely weren't dull. After consideration, I'd decided to phase Bill out. But not yet.

"Tea? Coffee? Actually, there's no milk."

"No problem. I'm a bit pushed for time anyway. Shall we?"

He headed towards the bedroom. As usual he took his clothes off quickly, so that he could watch me. Bill stood in his socks, and as I looked at him I thought of sweaty Wombles. It was more than his having a big nose and being hairy, it had something to do with the way he moved. To voice my thoughts didn't seem wise. He sat on the bed to watch me. I knew he enjoyed this, so I was careful to put on a show.

Once undressed I felt less exposed. This was my domain. Naked was my uniform. It had the advantage of taking away outward signs of my character, allowing punters the luxury of seeing me simply as a sex object. One of the things I liked about being naked was that it didn't look scruffy or smart, so there was no pressure to conform. I lay on my bed so that Bill could see the product: my chest, armpits, torso, abs, face, and crotch. To tease him, I turned my legs out just enough so that my thighs thickened and the tip of my of my bum crack showed. Over the years, if only to a certain extent, I'd learned to dissociate my body from my mind, enabling me to leave myself to Bill's enjoyment. Still, I kept part of my attention on him, checking to make sure he didn't cross any of my boundaries. I could expect some things he did to feel good, because physically they felt much the same no matter who enacted them. Some customers really got off on making me feel good, but my pleasure never concerned Bill.

I felt the likely wet sensation when he came to my crotch, accompanied by his mouth noises, and didn't tell him his teeth scratched. He worked his way slowly up my torso to my neck. I smelled his saliva. He was aware of the cutoff point, my face, and knew my lips were reserved for when I was intimate with somebody (or when I had *real* sex). Bill hovered around my borderline, doing things he knew were wrong but not actually crossing into the danger zone. This was part of our usual dynamic. He put his fingers near my bum hole and I maneuvered away. When he persisted I responded by getting off the bed, acting as though I was being sexy. I faced him, gave him a cocky expression, then turned around and backed onto the bed, kneeling, my thighs either side of his head and my bum just above his face—his favorite position. My balls dangled on his mouth. He made a snuffling action at my scrotum.

He was ready. I leaned over and reached for his dick. After half a dozen jerks, he came.

A moment later, Bill said, "Can I use the bathroom?"

"Sure," I said, forcing a smile, wanting him gone. Bill made a similar face. I assumed he didn't like me.

As he left the room I spoke after him. "What are you doing for the rest of the day?"

He mumbled something about Manchester. Finished in the bathroom, Bill dressed quickly, gave me two neatly folded twenty-pound notes, and left in the same sweaty, bothered state as he'd arrived. With some punters I'd have minded that they weren't relaxed or at least convinced they'd had sex, but with Bill I didn't. Our mutual disregard for each other was part of our currency.

I turned on the cassette player, using one of my knuckles in case there was any of Bill's cum on my hand. Relieved that he was gone and I was alone, I felt the need to put something back into me after he'd insidiously managed to take so much. I sat back on my bed and listened to a new Irish singer named Sinead O'Connor, losing myself in her banshee-like, soulful, and angry wailing, staring into the layers of surface created by the iridescence of the blue wall. It was 12:58. After about five minutes I

washed my hands and began to get ready for my shift. I anticipated feeling like shit for a few days.

– **2** –

The tube was busy and so I stood leaning against the doors.
Damn, I'd forgotten my book. No matter. I didn't like to read
standing up. It was the same with kissing and fucking. When the
goal was to lose myself totally I didn't like to have to concentrate
on complex things like being vertical or balance.

With several stops to my destination, Green Park station, I
decided to people-watch. For some reason, today everybody
looked like types, caricatures, even parodies of what they were
supposed to be. The woman beside me wore a brightly colored,
striped cardigan in need of a good washing. She smelled of piss.
A suited man with a smart shirt and tie attempted, within such
cramped conditions, to read his newspaper. Beside him was a gap,
and next to that a young man who was blind. He must have a dog;
hence the gap. The businessman took advantage of the empty
space to open his paper fully. As he did this he looked directly at
me, long enough to be communicating something. He was probably a former customer. By the time we reached my stop I was
glad to get off.

I headed towards Piccadilly, past the Ritz Hotel. At the third
street on the left I turned onto Old Bond Street and at the end of
the first block I turned right, into the doorway of the Burlington.
The dark, wood-paneled hallway, lined with gilt-framed mirrors,
reached deep into the building. All the fixtures and fittings were
brass. The carpet had a sensible pattern in gray, navy blue, and
maroon. At the end of hall was a doorway with a doorman. His
name was Steve, but we called him Sleeve.

"Hey, Sleeve," I greeted him.

"How's it going, fella?"

A quiet man, Sleeve didn't waste a smile unless he felt it, or speak unless he meant it. Anybody who didn't know him would probably think he looked mean, as I did when I first saw him. Sleeve had dark stubble that started below his neckline. It was thick on his face and blended smoothly with his tight-cropped hair. There was something *real bloke* about him.

"All right," I said. "Is it busy down there?"

"It's getting that way."

"How was your weekend?"

Sleeve scratched his neck, thinking. "Not bad," he said. He patted his head slowly and rubbed it. "There was something else . . . Oh yeah, it was your birthday. You were twenty-three. I forgot, didn't I?"

"It's nothing," I said.

"Sorry I didn't come out. I was doing the DJ thing."

"It's no big deal."

"How can you say that? The number twenty-three is very significant in numerology, especially for a man."

Numerology? Suddenly I lost interest in chatting.

"Just pulling your pisser." Sleeve grinned. "You should have seen your face."

"Wanker!" I said.

"Actually," said Sleeve like a shifty market trader, "I happen to know that wanking's your specialty."

"It's all my speciality."

His face took on a cartoon detective expression. "I know. I hear the rumors about you."

"In that case you should be scared. I've got to go. I'll catch you later."

I hurried downstairs. Luckily there was nobody on the front desk to scold me for being late, although in the kitchen just behind a partition I heard Sandy's loud, camp, thick Welsh accent. As quietly as I could I made my way quickly to the claustrophobic locker room that always smelled of deodorant, cigar smoke, and dirty socks. Lockers on each side reached up to the low ceiling. All the little doors made me think of *Alice in Wonderland*. I changed into my work clothes: black rugby shorts, football socks, and a white vest—I felt this looked "old school" and masculine—and headed into the hallway with its floor-to-ceiling smoked mirrors.

Apart from the small mirrors for shaving in the toilets, all surfaces in the Burlington that could possibly reflect how a customer really looked were smoked. The lounge, consisting of four small rooms that had been made into one, had a dozen wicker chairs with beige cushioned seats, set around four smoked-glass coffee tables. The chair and table legs, previously white, were covered in wavy lines of dark varnish meant to give the illusion of actual wood—which only worked in low lighting, from a distance, if you squinted. At the Burlington we always kept the lights dimmed. This was to make the customers feel more comfortable when sitting around only in towels, and it had the bonus of making the cream-colored carpet look clean-ish. Another room, located off one of the corners of the lounge, had a TV that showed porn nonstop. Unsurprisingly, it was even less well lit, as Burlington customers didn't want others to see them resorting to watching porn.

I glanced around the lounge to see if anything needed my attention. I picked up a stray towel hanging off one of the chairs and put it in the towel bin. The boys did things like this. It made us appear hardworking and keen to serve the customers. In reality, it was an opportunity to let customers see we were there, and get a close-up look at us in motion. I headed to the bar and stepped up onto it. Although the lighting was harsh, everybody could see you easily and it tended to be the focus of the lounge. It was easier to show off from there and flirt with customers. The boys referred to it as the stage.

One of the boys, S, was already mid-performance. His real name was Steve, the same as the doorman. To differentiate them, one had become Sleeve and the other S, *S* being short for S Child.

"Hi, you," he said, looking pleased to see me.

"Hello, S. Why so happy, smiley boy?"

"Why not?" he said.

"Good answer."

"Do you fancy a coffee?"

"Please. I had a hard weekend."

"I'm guessing you mean partying, not working?"

"A bit of both," I said. "Or maybe it was a *lot* of both. It was hard to tell which sometimes."

"Sounds fun. I think."

"It was. I think."

We both laughed.

"You mean you don't know?" said S, feigning shock.

"How would I?"

"You were there, weren't you?"

"Only in body."

"In that case I'm sure everybody had a good time. And I mean *everybody*."

I started to tickle S. "You cheeky bugger."

"Stop!" he squealed. Remembering his work persona, he dropped the tone of his voice an octave. "Stop."

"Steady on, boys," said a voice.

A frail-looking, older gentleman with his towel pulled up over his belly stood at the other side of the counter.

"I'm sorry," I said.

"We were just . . ." said S.

"I'm only fooling," said the man, wafting his hand as if to dismiss what he'd said. "Don't mind me. After all, boys will be boys. They like a bit of rough and tumble."

S clocked the man's taste in an instant. "That's right. I'll wrestle him later."

"Wrestle, hey?" said the man, his eyes focusing somewhere left of our heads.

Guessing that he was picturing us wrestling naked, I smiled as best I could, whereas S blossomed. He was one of the most popular boys in the club. Of course his full bum, chunky uncut dick, and Pre-Raphaelite curly hair helped. More than all of these, I think it was because he was so good with the customers. He knew how to work them, and he had a nice attitude. When I first met S, I'd thought him sweet, almost childlike, even vacant. As I spent more time with him, I discovered his Buddha-like simplicity. He was never judgmental and seemed to undermine negativity—rare qualities.

"Would you like anything, sir?" he said.

"I'll take a pot of tea, please."

"What kind would you like? English Breakfast?"

"You wouldn't by any chance happen to have Earl Grey?"

"Certainly, sir. Milk or lemon?"

"Lemon, please."

"Coming right up. Do you fancy something to nibble on, sir?" S opened his arms. "Something sweet, maybe?" With his palms facing the man, he added coyly. "We have a selection of buns."

"Why not?" said the man. "A chocolate one would be splendid."

"You take a seat and I'll bring over a selection. Won't be a minute, sir."

"Jolly good."

To make sure that the man left the bar area—and me—S paused to watch him turn and go to sit down, then darted into the kitchen.

As soon as S was out of sight the old man turned back, put both hands on the bar, and said to me, "I haven't seen you here before."

"I've just started."

This was the stock answer used by the boys in such situations. In fact, I'd been at the Burlington for months.

"What's your name?" I asked the man.

"Arthur. Art, if you like."

He offered me his hand.

"Hello, Art, good to meet you."

We shook formally.

"That's a fine handshake you have there, my boy."

"Thanks. They're laborer's hands." This wasn't a big lie; I'd used to work on a building site with my dad as a teenager during summer holidays.

"You're a builder, hey?"

"My dad taught me everything I know."

Arthur gazed into space again. I guessed he was imagining me on a building site, naked. Or me and my dad naked. Or just a mass of builders-plasterers-electricians-joiners naked, having a gang bang. His focus shifted back to me.

"I hope you're going to take full advantage of our equipment," I said, and without breaking eye contact gave my crotch a quick nudge. "The gym, I mean."

He looked me up and down, taking his time. His mouth fell into an O shape, his tongue twisted, and he squinted, giving him the comical look of a turtle.

"I know exactly what you meant," he said slowly, a mischievous look in his eyes. "And I jolly well intend to."

"It's the best equipment in the city," I teased.

"It is, is it?"

"Well, let me know if I can do anything for you."

"Actually, I was hoping you could give me a hand . . ." He paused and smiled, using an expression that I believe was intended to look shrewd but actually looked inane. This he held for two seconds, and then continued, ". . . with something."

"I'd be happy to. Just let me know."

S reappeared from the kitchen, but he was too late. Now he was just some boy with tea and biscuits.

"And your name?" Art asked me.

"Aiden."

Art said something about my name, but I was more concerned with S watching us. I stepped down from the stage. To give S another chance, I made a vague excuse to Art and left S to it, confident that Art would book *me* for a massage later.

Art's posh, lacy laugh clung to me as I walked down the hallway.

— **3** —

After working the streets, the sea front, pubs, and toilets, and advertising in the gay press in Brighton, I had moved to London and got my own place. I worked in a similar way, hanging around Piccadilly Circus, and also put an ad in the *Pink Paper*. There were only about six of us advertising then, so we were able to charge a lot. But the work was sporadic and I had to do it whenever it presented itself. Cubus had stayed behind to finish his degree at Brighton Polytechnic, then came to London. We had begun working at the Burlington because it was convenient. It provided a never-ending stream of punters. Then we got an apartment together.

Some days I hated the Burlington. It wasn't the massage oil, which permeated everything in my home via contaminated work clothes. Nor was it the coffee, trucked down from Liverpool and shipped from Japan, its origin Costa Rica. It wasn't even saliva and cum, as some might expect. More likely it was the mix of eucalyptus, musty cellar, bleach, and musk that went through my nostrils to my throat, and into my mouth.

There was an eerie stillness to the place today. The lounge was particularly quiet. I headed towards the steam room, along the mirrored hallway that ran down the side of the gym area.

"Hey, Gary," I said to the instructor showing somebody how to use the machines.

He looked over. "Aiden!"

His voice always sounded warm and welcoming and a bit rehearsed. He was with a client, so the conversation ended there. Even when he wasn't busy, we never did more than relay what each of us had done at the weekend.

Gary was striking, like a 1970s TV detective. Oddly, I never heard anybody mention his good looks. This may have been because he did not do massages. If customers wanted to interact with him they had to go through the motions of working out.

At the end of the hallway I arrived at massage room one. Between the door and its frame was a wad of tissue. This served two purposes. It secured the door, jamming it shut, and it indicated that somebody was working inside the room. I tried to imagine who it might be. Around the corner, to my right, the doors to rooms two and three were open. I looked in them to check that they were clean and there was enough oil for massaging, alcohol for wiping off the oil, and tissue for mopping up all sorts of fluid. Just past rooms two and three was the sauna, which was always empty, mainly because it was well-lit and hot. Opposite this was the steam room, where it was the boys' responsibility to make sure nobody had sex. My gut feeling was that it was busy. I hesitated and prepared myself, then opened the glass door. It was so steamy that it was difficult to see anything, but once the cloud escaped through the open door all became clearer.

About thirty men packed the room, so much wet, pink skin moving and limbs recoiling amid the smell of Olbas oil. All the familiar characters were there: Hirsute Harry, Tepid-Tea Tim, Lick-a-Lot Leonard. They usually had their favorite seats, but today everybody was focused on the same point in the room. As their hands moved away I saw the source of all the excitement: about nine chunky, uncut inches standing stiff against the belly-button of an abdomen with perfect hair distribution, attached to the most magnificent-looking man I'd seen in a long time. Either I overly admired the male of our species or I met an improbable amount of godlike men. Technically there were many incredible specimens in the world. Their being susceptible to my gravitational pull was perhaps somewhat implausible, but regardless, I was fucking lucky. Actually, I believe it was more likely that I was simply really appreciative of men, probably stemming from once feeling I was so unlike them and never quite believing that they would notice me, let alone take a second look, and definitely not want to touch, kiss, or fuck with me. Admittedly I was hyperaware of many things, from the translucence of an aphid to the feel of getting naked between cool cotton sheets on a summer evening to the smell on the head of a month-old baby.

I made my way towards the back wall, to do as the management instructed in such situations, trying to act professional. This was difficult, as the room was so full. I had to brush past slippery bodies packed in around me the whole way. It was like rush hour on the underground—but naked, sweatier, with everybody even more eager to get off. Men placed towels over their crotches and coughed conspicuously. Instead of distracting me, it drew my attention to them.

The stranger with the big dick was probably a tourist who had wandered in clueless, but he didn't seem to mind the attention. It wouldn't have taken long for all the customers in the club to become aware of his presence. Some would have heard about him, others would have seen him enter. The canny would simply have known there was a new man in the vicinity. On such occasions, everybody crushed into the steam room in the hope of rubbing up against him. His proximity alone excited them. This feeding frenzy behavior occurred whenever there was a big dick in the club. The bigger it was, the less it mattered what the man attached to it looked like.

Finally I reached the back wall of the steam room. "Afternoon, gents!" I said, using my "police constable" voice.

"Afternoon," said Big-Dicked Stranger.

I took an instant liking to him for being bold. Normally nobody replied.

"Having fun there, mister?" I challenged.

"Would if you joined us," he said.

A rumble of laughter broke the reverent silence.

"Somebody's got a sense of humor," I said. "I'm here to stop you guys fooling around, not encourage it, but I can see what everybody's so excited about."

"I'm flattered," said the man.

"And I'm not against fun. But in the eyes of the law this steam room's a public place. We don't want to get shut down now, do we?"

The Burlington billed itself as a gentlemen's health club, and for the sake of appearances all the boys were required to be legally licensed as professional masseurs. As far as the owners were concerned, I suspected that the ban on sex in the steam room had more to do with money than indecency, since much of what actually happened at the Burlington was illegal. People getting off in the steam room meant the owners would lose the profits they made from massages. The boys' concern was also financial, as the club didn't pay us anything for giving massages and only a minimal fee per shift. We made our real money from "extras." These could be as elaborate as the boys' imaginations allowed—and every boy was guilty of stretching the boundaries at some time or another—but usually it was a simple hand job.

When I opened the steam room door to leave, somebody grasped my wrist. "So what's your name?" said a stubbly mouth close to my ear.

A small chorus of men said, "Aiden Shaw!" Several of them laughed.

I turned to find Big-Dicked Stranger close behind me, near enough for me to notice water trickle, stop, and drip off the end of his strong yet pretty nose. I took hold of the knot at the front of the towel he'd put around him, and pulled it. My dick pulsed.

"Do you mind stepping out of here?" I said.

"Sure," he said.

I closed the door behind us. Before he could say anything, I pressed my mouth against his.

"Thank you," he said. "What was that for?"

"For noticing me. For leaving that room. For being cocky. For having such defined red lips."

He pushed his wet beige hair into shape with his fingers. "So many reasons."

"I'm just getting started," I said. "But I could fill you in later." I glanced up and down the corridor. "Do you fancy going for a drink when I finish here?"

"I don't drink, but I'll happily watch you."

"Write down your number and slide it into my locker,

number twenty-two. I'll call you as soon as I'm done here. You got all that?"

"Sure."

"What locker number?"

"Twenty-two."

"Good man. I've got to carry on now, but . . ." I took hold of his hand and put it on my crotch.

"Wow!"

"It's *your* fault."

"I take full responsibility," he said. "And will take it like a man."

"Funny," I said, and kissed him again. "Gotta go now."

I turned, then paused to watch him dry himself.

"Hey, handsome," I said.

He looked up.

"What's your name?"

"Love."

"Are you serious?"

"My parents were hippies," I said.

He shuffled from one foot to the other, looking adorably uncomfortable. I laughed.

"God bless them hippies."

"I'm from San Francisco."

"Cool. I've always wanted to go there."

"I'm sure they'd dig you there." He grinned. "Every single one of them, if they got the chance."

"I'd wear them out."

"Sounds hot." It seemed he believed my act.

"I was just kidding," I said. "I'd need to go twice to get through the whole city." I winked at him.

"Stud!"

"You'll see."

I turned and continued on to the far end of the hall where the showers faced the toilet area. My job there was to make sure the soap dispensers were full and there was enough toilet paper in the stalls. This section of the club had a particularly furtive feel to it. Perhaps this was a specifically gay thing. Toilets were a place where men stood with their dicks out, next to other men with their dicks on display, which automatically meant sex to some people. Whenever I entered the room the men would tuck themselves back into their towels, whatever their state of arousal, which was fine by me.

When I got back to the lounge, S said, "Room two. Guess who."

"Art?"

"It seems you charmed the towel off him."

I smiled.

The standard issue for a massage session was two towels, one to place on the bench, a hygiene thing, and the other to cover the customer's private parts. Not that anybody ever wanted to do this; even if they didn't want extras, customers always seemed to want to expose themselves to the boys. It didn't matter to me if they did. After a few weeks at the Burlington I barely noticed, unless there was something extraordinary on view. Usually it appeared to be like any other body part, and my mind was on doing everything in my power to convince the customer he wanted the relief that extras could bring. If, however, I saw his dick move or swell, no matter how slightly, it piqued my interest, as it was quite likely work would ensue.

I picked up the towels at the front desk, tucked them under my arm, and walked confidently into massage room one.

Damn! One of the other boys, Kydd, was on top of the bench, squatting over a customer's face.

"Sorry!" I said. "Wrong room."

I turned to the correct room this time, but first stopped to knock.

"Art?" I inquired.

"Yes," he said. "Come in, come in."

By now I sensed he was well aware of his innuendos.

"It'll be my pleasure," I said—why pretend we weren't playing that game?—and entered the room, then jammed a thick wad of tissue in the door, and kicked it firmly shut behind me.

The first thing I saw was my own reflection, in the mirror on the opposite wall—which unfortunately told me that my mood had swung from feeling good about Art choosing me to the reality of actually doing him. That would be the E I took at the weekend. Snap out of it, Aiden, I silently ordered myself.

"How do you like it, then, Art?"

"Just be gentle with me!"

The tone of his voice told me what he really wanted. "I don't do gentle," I said. "I'm a fuckin' paddy-builder, mate."

"Gracious me! Please don't hurt me."

I whacked his bum, but not hard; it was clear he didn't want real pain, just the intimation of a fantasy. Anyway, I couldn't start anything too early in the session. If I did, I'd run out of things to do and say. Besides, I had to keep quiet. I'd learned from experience that it was embarrassing when people outside the room heard what was going on.

I started Art's massage, keeping it gentle. Beyond the SM playacting, I assumed that what he truly wanted was the same as most customers: It didn't really matter to them how sex-like the scenario was as long as somebody noticed, heard, and above all, touched them. Much like a hairdresser, I had to gauge how much of these things the customer needed.

Pale green woodchip paper covered the walls. Apart from random patches of shiny gloss, it was painted with matte emulsion. Since working at the Burlington I'd come in pretty fucked up at times. Once, on acid, while giving a massage to a particularly vile customer named Benjamin I looked up and saw reflections of light on every single chip of wood. They looked as though they were sparkling. Amazed by the intricacy and complexity of the surface, I stared. Then I looked down at Benjamin's dick, which seemed agitated. I thought of cattle just before they're slaughtered. When I looked up again the wall was covered in bugs, thousands of them. Eventually I convinced myself I was tripping and the chips weren't insects. The trouble was that, briefly, I'd thought of my mum, and wondered what she'd think if she could see me attempting to conjure up a hard-on from somebody I didn't even like. Among the boys Benjamin had the reputation for always trying to get more than we were prepared to give, and always for less than we'd normally charge. It didn't matter what price we asked. He always knocked it down, especially if he knew we needed the money. My guess was that it was less about getting a bargain than about exercising power. Once more I looked up. Now the room was crying. Every chip had become a tear. It looked beautiful, like Jesus did when being crucified.

Art was blissing out. Massaging him with one hand, with my other hand I moved the clock on the wall forward ten minutes. Art had only booked half an hour; there wasn't much time left. I pressed my crotch against his face, squashing my dick and balls against his mouth.

"So, cocksucker," I said, "my balls are ready to pop." My acting hadn't improved since my school days; my voice vacillated between American movie cowboy and Mancunian manual laborer.

"Oh, dear," Art said, as though scripted.

"My girlfriend'll want a good drillin' when I get home tonight."

"She's a lucky lady."

"She's no *lady*, but that's another story. Meanwhile, cocksucker, you gonna get me off first or what? I'm horny as a fuck dog."

"Oh! I don't know," he said, concern in his voice. "I wasn't expecting . . ."

"I don't give a damn what you expected." I tapped into the lingo I'd heard in American porn movies. "You got me all wound up and now you're gonna take my huge fuckin' load." It sounded just as silly when *I* said it, and even as I spoke I sensed it wasn't working. Still, it was a tried and tested formula. "You lisnin?"

"I'm listening," he said, sparrow-like, sounding truly scared.

"And you betta be as good as all those spunky laborers on the building site."

"I don't know," he said.

He sat up on the bench abruptly, then stood and pulled his towel over his belly and chest area the way a woman would.

I paused. "So, are you gonna have extras or am I gonna have to whack your arse again?" I said. "I warn you, this time I won't hold back."

"The massage was splendid," Art said, attempting to smile. It crumpled into a frail frown. Suddenly I was aware how old he must feel, how vulnerable and fragile.

"Don't worry," I said gently, my voice now sincere and careful. "I'm not really going to hurt you."

It was too late. Art was already backing out of the room, with remarkable speed for such an old man.

I had a funny feeling in my gut, possibly anxiety. Not because I was going to get into trouble—as one of the most frequently requested masseurs, I could get away with a lot. It wasn't that difficult to convince the receptionist that the customer had either misunderstood, tried to take advantage, or crossed the Burlington's unspoken boundaries. Something else bothered me. As I wiped down the bench with alcohol I paused, contemplating how I might have scared poor old Art. I continued to clean, spending more time than usual wiping the surface of the bench carefully, swiftly stroking the legs, and rubbing smudges off the mirror. Just before leaving the room I reset the clock, careful to leave the door ajar at a forty-five-degree angle.

This last action didn't relate directly to Art but was some kind of neurosis I had begun to develop. The room was now perfectly ready for the next client: vacant, clean, and available. I thought of Art. Although sometimes cheaper than we'd like, *available* shouldn't be confused with *free*.

— **4** —

"Psst, Cubus!" I whispered loud enough for him to hear me.

"What?" he snapped. But then he gave me a greeting-card smile.

"Knock him dead, Boy Wonder," I said.

"Believe me," he said, "there's nothing I'd like more to do to this prick."

"You know him?"

Cubus fluttered an imaginary fan in front of his face. "I've *known* him," he said coquettishly, backing into massage room one. He closed the door.

Massage room three was my least favorite. It was long and narrow, which made it difficult to get around the table without pressing up against the punter. If he didn't want extras, all that body contact was like giving him a freebee.

I thought of Art's hasty retreat. I'd already prepared my cover story, in case Sandy, the obnoxious queen on reception, questioned me. Art had wanted me to do something unspeakable. We were all pretty forthright, if not crude, so I couldn't imagine what might possibly be *unspeakable*, but that was the story I was going to stick to. I'd leave it up to Sandy's imagination.

The washing machine was in the kitchen. I went there with

the dirty towels. The kitchen had a cork notice board covered with notes for the boys. I noticed a half-eaten protein bar one of the boys must have nibbled before rushing in to do a massage. Empty milk bottles sat in crates. Mousetraps lay tucked subtly beside the washer, fridge, cooker, and dryer.

Kydd was crouching, ready to start the washing machine. The terra cotta floor tiles contrasted with his faded green shorts and candy blue eyes.

"Hold on, let me throw these towels in," I said.

He smiled. "No problem."

I squatted on my haunches at his level. There was nowhere to sit in the kitchen, which was probably intentional. Kydd leaned one elbow on a shelf with nothing on it but a dead cactus. Stuck in the hard gray mud beside it a plastic Santa waved, oblivious to context.

"Cheers," I said.

I'd known Kydd since Brighton Polytechnic, before he had plastic surgery. I'd met many people who'd had things resized, removed, or reshaped, but Kydd's was the most successful I'd ever seen. He could have been a poster boy for cosmetic enhancement. Although both of us were articulate, communication between us was patchy, perhaps because I'd known him before he had a neat nose, a comic book jaw, and an LA set of teeth. (He'd always had bright blond hair and blue eyes.)

"Sorry about the intrusion," I said. "I mean *mine*, not his tongue."

Kydd laughed. "Funny bastard. It was my stupid fault for forgetting the tissue in the door."

"I always dread doing that," I said.

"You mean to say, there are things that Aiden Shaw minds people seeing him do?"

"Sure, like giving a massage"—I grabbed my crotch in a

AIDEN SHAW

macho way—"*without* extras. How embarrassing would that be? I'm not some New Age healer. I'm a fucking whore."

"*Fucking* being the operative word."

"Well, I'm not a *sucking* whore," I said.

"Aiden, you're a trip!"

"So ride me."

We looked at each other, him possibly wondering if I meant what I'd said and me for the first time realizing I might have. We both registered something.

He pressed the washing machine start button and stood up. "That feels like the first thing I've turned on all day," he said.

"Are you telling me that sitting on that punter's face didn't turn him on?"

"Lord, is that how it seemed? You got it all wrong. I was just resting."

"If only sitting around were always so well paid."

Kydd flashed his perfect teeth, looking genuinely happy. Then his expression changed.

"Aiden, I know this is a bit of a funny question, but you haven't seen any football cards around, have you?"

"I have, actually. They're at the front desk. I saw them next to the coffee machine, and gave them to Sandy. They're yours?"

"My godson's."

"You're let near children?"

"I *babysit* him," he said.

"Please don't tell me you get paid for *more* sitting."

"I do, actually, but I put the money in an account for him. My sister doesn't know. She doesn't even know I'm gay."

"How Fifties."

"Tell me about it."

"Can't she tell?"

He folded a pile of clean towels. "She asked why all my friends are good-looking, fit, and male."

"That's easy, just tell her they attract better-looking girls."

"I'm way ahead of you. Once she saw me with a customer in the Versace shop."

S popped his head around the door. "Baby," he said, looking at me. "Cheese sandwich. *Loads* of pickle."

"No problem. Is it for Lard Arse? He always wants extra something, but never extras."

S rolled his eyes. "I know," he said, and gave me a sweet *please* expression.

For that lovely face alone, I pulled the bread, cheese, and butter out of the fridge and started to make the sandwich. S disappeared.

I returned my attention to Kydd. "Shit," I said, "busted with a punter in Versace. How embarrassing. *Versace!* Of all places. How did you get out of that one?"

"She thought I was doing charity work with old folks."

"She doesn't know how charitable you really are with the old folks."

"Well, it's hardly free, is it?"

"True, but you're such a giving person."

"Bitch!" he said, laughing. He fiddled with the drawstring of his shorts, absentmindedly stroking the golden hairs just above his crotch. His belly stuck out slightly. Only when we were "behind the scenes" did he relax and let this happen. It made him look boyish, which he could have used as a selling point, but I thought better than to let him know I'd noticed it.

There was no pickle in the fridge. I crouched down beside Kydd to get it from the cupboard, where we stored it. Now his tummy was at my eye level, those soft hairs nearer my face. How warm his skin would be just there, under his belly button. Could

I somehow feel the heat and weight of him beside me? Did I truly fancy Kydd? How weird.

Cubus stomped into the kitchen, disgruntled. I felt like I'd been caught doing something.

"That was quick," I said, standing up.

"Yeah, he's a pain in the neck but doesn't last long. Thank god."

With a jar of pickles in one hand, I put my arm around him, "How was it with Javier?" I said. I had to turn my back on him to continue with the sandwich.

"Good." He paused. "I guess."

"Was this the boy from Saturday?" Kydd asked.

"Yeah," I said, craning my neck to address them both.

"The first few hours were," Cubus continued.

Now he had us intrigued.

"But . . . ?" said Kydd. "What happened?"

"Nothing. How should I put it? He just passed his sell-by date. He expired."

Kydd and I laughed. "Harsh!" said Kydd.

"Poor boy," I said, still facing the sandwich. "You've just had it too good, too often."

Cubus sashayed in beside me, turning his face towards mine, a little too close for comfort. He blew on his nails as though drying the polish on them. "Maybe I have. Maybe I haven't," he said.

Taking hold of a bread knife, I said, "And what does Kyle think of it all?"

"He doesn't know."

"Oh, lord," I said, shaking my head exaggeratedly like some righteous gossip from church.

I cut through the sandwich and, chore finished, nipped out to the lounge. S was leaning on the counter. "Here you go," I said. "One pickle sandwich with cheese."

Lard Arse chuckled. He gave me his version of a saucy look. I reversed into the kitchen, playing the servant and smiling. Within seconds, S followed me.

"He wants *you*," he said, without a trace of resentment.

"Sorry, Star-child." I said. "I wasn't trying to work him. The opposite, in fact."

S made a funny face, which meant *it's okay*. Trying to make him feel better, I asked if he wanted coffee.

"No thanks, Shady."

Even at school, nobody ever gave me nicknames. I was always just Aiden. I liked it that S did. Everyone tended to call him anything beginning with S. It made him smile, which was always a lovely sight.

"You okay?" I said.

"I'm having a bit of a gray day."

"Join the gang," said Cubus. "What drug caused yours?"

"Just several big fault lines," S said, and mimed snorting some drug.

"That'll shift your tectonic plates," said Kydd, sounding overly educated. Nobody responded but me, as I liked wordplay.

"You're lucky you didn't flatline," I said.

My comment evoked a minor snicker from Cubus.

"Sorry!" I said cringing. "I kind of tore the arse out of that joke, didn't I?"

Everybody turned to look at a tiny mouse that scurried along the floor between the cooker and fridge.

S smiled. "If I did OD, I wouldn't have to come in to work," he said.

"That'd be dead lucky," I said.

Everyone groaned, and so I shut up.

At the end of my shift and several clients later, I took the pile of money from my sock—that was where all the boys stored it—showered, changed out of my uniform, and went up to the street to wait for Cubus, who was dealing with a last-minute booking.

It felt good to be aboveground. Even the London air felt fresh. The street was quiet. I called Love from a phone box on the street and arranged to meet him at ten o'clock in a pub in Soho called the Golden Lion.

I leaned against a wall and pulled out the book that S had loaned me earlier in the week, *Siddhartha* by Herman Hesse. It gripped me and sucked me straight back in.

A yellow sports car pulled up, its horn honking. Inside was Benjamin, everybody's least favorite client. The window slid down.

"What are you doing with the trash, Aiden?"

"I'm not *with* the trash," I said. "I'm *beside* it."

"Whichever," he said, his window going up as he drove off.

Cubus was out shortly. We were the last to leave the Burlington, besides the manager. As always we headed into Soho to unwind over coffee in Bar Italia and, just like we normally did, vented our comedowns from the weekend. Only something was different.

"Just to remind you, Cubus, we haven't got long," I said. "I've got that outcall at the Ritz. But we can talk at home properly tonight."

"I thought I told you," Cubus said. "Mark Lawrence is going to Thailand for three months and he's asked me to look after his flat."

"I don't remember you saying anything," I told Cubus, and paused. Giving him the benefit of the doubt, I added, "Maybe you told me on Saturday. I never remember anything when I'm high."

"That'll be it. Anyway, I'm staying at his place for a few days before he goes, to get used to it. I'll collect some stuff from our flat over the next week."

Hearing this made me jealous. In addition to working at the Burlington, Mark Lawrence was another of Cubus's shags. I fancied him but he never showed any interest in me other than friendship. A bit weirded out, I carried on as usual. We counted the money we'd made. I had two hundred and fifty pounds. Cubus had a record three hundred, plus thirty-three dollars some American had passed off on him.

Shocked, I said, "Fucking hell!"

"I sure hope so. Cause hell's bound to be where I end up."

Fine by me, I thought, even though I was an atheist. This response was bitchier than I ordinarily allowed myself to be. But I could have sworn that Cubus was gloating that he'd made more than I had, maybe because I usually made more than he did. Perhaps this was complicated by his unreturned sexual feelings for me. I didn't have time to give this much thought, as I had an outcall at the Ritz that would bring in at least another hundred and fifty.

— **5** —

The Ritz Hotel was grand, sophisticated, and established, unlike me. The only thing we had in common was façade. Mine may not have been as ornate but it was equally phony. I was presenting myself as an escort; I advertised as one, negotiated like one on the phone, and I identified as one to whoever was interested. I even simulated sex for escort rates.

For today's performance I wore a buttoned-up pale blue cotton shirt, a navy cashmere V-neck sweater, and cream trousers, all by Ralph Lauren. My disguise was a costume intended to help me pass as respectable. How would anybody know I was scum? When I wasn't working at the Burlington, most of the time I dressed "properly," in case I had an outcall. So I felt quite confident going up to the concierge's desk.

"Hello," I said, as though I was just a nephew visiting my uncle. "I'm here to see Mr. Boden. Gerrick Boden." When I was sixteen I'd learned about Method acting at school. Although I didn't actually have any memories of visiting a family member in a posh hotel, I tried to find a source to tap into.

"Certainly, sir," said the concierge. I expected a glance up and down, but no. His eyes, although heavy, looked at me as if he were taller than I was. "Who shall I say is here?"

"Aiden," I said, thinking the name didn't sound anything like a rentboy's. "He's expecting me."

The concierge placed his thumb and forefinger into his waistcoat pocket and picked up the receiver with the other hand. He held the handset so comfortably, it might have been part of him. "One moment," he said, his gaze reaching the corner of the high ceiling, his nostrils flexing. "Good evening, Mr. Boden, this is your concierge, Fletcher."

Fletcher. The title *concierge* suited him equally well. His slicked-back hair looked painted on his head.

"There is a gentleman here with me in the reception who wishes to see you, a Mr. Aiden. Would you like to speak to him?"

"That's Mr. Shaw," I said.

"I'm sorry, sir," Fletcher said into the receiver. "Would you excuse me a moment?" He cocked his head to one side and pushed an ear towards me, his face re-forming into a listening expression.

I played along. "My name's Aiden Shaw. *Aiden*'s my first name."

The concierge nodded to me. "Very well," he said, raising his eyes to the ceiling again. He spoke into the receiver. "Forgive me, sir, I stand corrected. The gentleman's name is Mr. Shaw." He paused. "Very good, sir. Right away."

Fletcher brought his line of vision down to me. "Mr. Boden would like you to go up to his room," he said.

"Thank you." I smiled, more *at* him than *to* him.

Possibly sensing the fun I was having at his expense, he said, "I trust you know where the lifts are."

"Yes," I said, but really I had no idea.

"Very good, sir." He continued as before, impervious, unconcerned, or simply not interested. "It's on the second floor. Take a left out of the lift and at the end of the hallway you'll find Room 141. I hope you enjoy your visit here at London's Ritz Hotel, and that you'll take full advantage of all our facilities." He spoke as though reading the stock employee welcome from a card, with a stale expression of servitude that fitted the verse perfectly. Fortunately he gestured the direction of the elevators with a flat hand.

I thanked him again and headed that way. Floor two, left, end of hallway. I knocked on the door three times.

"Just a second," said a muffled voice from inside Room 141.

The door opened slowly, revealing a man in a wheelchair with a look of deep concentration on his face. Why hadn't he mentioned his disability? I was shocked and annoyed, but tried not to show either as I attempted to process the unexpected information. My mind was a mass of questions. What would this situation entail? How would I navigate his wheelchair? Might he want to get out of it? Should I offer to help him? Most importantly, would any of this affect my hard-on?

There was a pause as we evaluated each other. I felt deceived. I shifted my focus, trying to see anything but the wheelchair. He wore an expensive-looking polo-neck jumper and well-tailored trousers. Despite his trendy-older-man designer clothes he had the humble appearance of a woodcutter in a fairy tale, with four-inch-long hair that looked like long fiber optics and looped around a five-inch bald spot on top of his head. He must have been Nordic in origin.

"I'm sorry," he said finally, as though suddenly remembering protocol. "Come in, come in."

I remembered how I was supposed to behave. "Thank you. . . . I'm Aiden."

With some difficulty he wheeled himself backwards, to make way for me. I walked through the door past him and into a lounge area. My first thought was of how expensive the suite must have been to hire. The decor reminded me of every other fancy hotel I'd visited over the last few years: luxurious, opulent, and ugly. He motioned for me to sit on a sofa covered with cream fabric woven in shiny and matte stripes.

"I'm Gerrick, Aiden," he said once I'd settled. He had trouble maneuvering his wheelchair. I felt uncomfortable. "I can't get used to this damn . . ." After a moment, he seemed to find the spot he sought. "It's not a permanent thing, you understand."

I tried to think of another topic.

"Where you from?"

"I'm American."

I rolled my eyes. "I did notice that much. I meant where *in* America?"

"Sorry. I'm from North Carolina." His expression was sweet, naïve. "You spotted the accent, huh?"

"Barely," I said, smiling.

"That's polite of you." He smiled back, looking suspicious. "Or were you being ironic? I can never tell with you Brits."

"I was."

"I should have known. Anyway, I gave up trying to lose the accent years ago, although it used to be much thicker than this. Can you believe it?"

"Sure. I like it," I said. "It sounds friendly."

"You think?"

"To my detriment."

"I'm sorry?" He looked confused.

"It's to my detriment that I think." I paused. "Sometimes."

Gerrick jerked his head back slightly. "That was a bright response."

"Sorry."

"You don't have to dumb down for me. I like a man with a good head on his shoulders."

"Good. I was only joking about the *sorry*."

"So you're a kidder, too." He looked pleased.

"I've been known to dredge out a joke now and then. I'm not saying anybody ever laughed, though."

"You're a funny one, Aiden."

"I hope you're not talking about this getup," I said, indicating my clothes.

"No. You carry it off well. I've met some boys . . . let's just say they didn't manage it so successfully."

"It sounds like you've a fairly good brain, too, Mr. Boden."

"Please call me Gerrick. I'm not at work now."

"Maybe so, but I am."

"Ouch!" He hunched his shoulders. "Okay, let's say you're not. I'm going to give you your money now. Here, take it. This way, you know I'm not wasting your time . . . and it doesn't matter if nothing happens."

He handed me three hundred pounds in fifty-pound notes.

"Thank you," I said. "That's generous."

"It's just money." He pinched his bottom lip between his forefinger and thumb, then pointed at me. "But *you're* special."

"That's a kind thing to say."

"I think it's true."

"How do you know what I am? We've only just met."

"Intuition, I guess. It's my best quality."

"Who says?"

"It's kind of what I'm known for at work."

"Hang on," I said. "We'll get back to that. But if I walked out of this room now, you're saying you'd be cool about that?"

"I'd be disappointed." He paused, looking genuine and slightly hurt. "But I don't think you would do that, Aiden. Do you know why?"

"I'd like to hear your version."

"First, you have integrity. Second, I interest you, and you probably want to see where this experience leads." He rubbed the skin on the top of his head with his hands and locked them in his hair, behind his neck. "I think you're a bit of a psychologist. Am I right about any of this?"

"I don't want to blow my own trumpet, but yes, I believe I have integrity. And yes, you interest me, which means you guessed right, I do want to see where this leads."

"And the psychologist bit?"

"I could do with seeing one."

"I don't think so. I think you do a good job of keeping check of yourself."

"Can I interrupt you a moment? I'm enjoying our conversation, and not just because you're saying nice things about me, but I know about the cream teas here."

"You read my mind. Scones with clotted cream?"

I nodded. "And strawberry jam."

"I knew there was something about you I liked." Gerrick reached for the telephone. "Pass me that, will you?"

I jumped up and did as he asked.

"Yes," he said into the receiver. "Could you bring up cream tea for two?" He looked at me, holding the receiver against his chest. "Sandwiches? They're very cute."

"Sure."

"And a selection of sandwiches, please." He was just about to hang up. "Hello? Sorry, one more thing. Could you bring extra clotted cream? Thank you."

Gerrick sat still, looking at the phone in his lap. He turned back to me.

"Is Aiden your real name?"

"Yes. I like it, and I've got nothing to hide."

"Very good. You *do* have integrity."

"Am I being interviewed?"

Gerrick smiled and shook his head.

I continued. "I've always tried to live by my own sense of right and wrong. I assume I learned this from my parents. Well, my mum."

"Interesting. If you don't mind me asking, what's your background?"

"I was brought up Catholic, if that's what you mean, a large family, and we were pretty poor."

Gerrick sighed; it seemed real.

"But back to you. You mentioned your work. Can I ask you about it?"

"Ask away."

"What kind of work do you do?"

"I work for Feehlar and Backard." He said this as though it was self-explanatory.

"What's that? Rather, what do they, or *you* do for them?"

"I'm the Executive Creative Director."

"Job titles aren't my strong point. I've never had a job in my life, apart from working with my dad on the building site."

"You're clearly bright."

"I went to college for a year, then I started doing this."

"Why do you still do it? You could easily get all sorts of work."

"It's my choice."

"Really?"

"I think so."

"Do you mean that?"

"I thought so," I said. "What do you think?"

"I don't know yet. I'm still trying to figure you out."

"Anyway, what do you actually do?"

"Feehlar and Backard is an advertising agency, and you could say I call the shots, creatively."

"Are they a big company?"

"They're probably the *best*."

"Impressive."

Gerrick laughed. "You're charming."

There was a knock at the door.

"That was quick," Gerrick said. "Will you get that?"

I opened the door. An elderly porter wheeled in a delicious-looking spread. He looked like he was from a bygone era.

"Where would you like the trolley, sir?" he said with decorum, as though he really believed in the role he played.

"Anywhere over there." Gerrick gestured to an exact point in the center of the room.

"Very good, sir." Slowly and carefully the porter placed it. "Will there be anything else, sir?"

"No," said Gerrick.

"Anything else for you, sir?" he said to me.

"No, thank you. Everything looks perfect." I smiled.

"Thank you, sir," he said, his manners impeccable, then turned, walked to the door, and closed it quietly behind him.

Gerrick and I looked at each other and burst out laughing.

"They're outrageous, aren't they?" he said.

"Very funny." I agreed. "I love it, though."

"Me, too."

We turned our attention to the trolley.

"Dig in, buddy!" said Gerrick. This didn't sound authentic coming from him, but if he was trying to make me feel comfortable, it worked. We continued to talk, our mouths full of sandwiches and jammy, cream-covered scones. "So, what excites you?" he said. "I'm guessing it's not sex."

"You are a clever man. I assume you want the truth, not some rentboy nonsense."

"Definitely."

"Well, I studied visual and performance art."

"Interesting."

"Perhaps, but in no way vocational."

"And so?"

"Actually, I prefer to write these days."

"No kidding. And this is the boy who never worked."

"Not at a proper job."

"I think you mean a *boring* job."

"I guess I do, or a job that I get paid for."

"You can get paid for writing."

"Like that's ever going to happen. Me a writer?"

"Is that what you'd like to be?"

"You mean, when I grow up?"

Gerrick laughed—a head-back, mouth-open laugh. He lifted his napkin to cover any half-chewed food.

"You seem pretty mature to me, but just for the fun of it, yes, tell me. What do you want to be when you grow up?"

I knew Gerrick enough already to know he would prefer a considered response, not something glib. My thoughts shifted to a more serious level. What *did* I want to be when I grew up?

"Sometimes I feel like the same boy I always was. Maybe I'll never grow up," I said.

"Maybe that's not a bad thing."

"That's a whole other conversation," I said. "But one thing at a time. If and when I do . . ." I paused a moment, then my first couple of answers came out quickly. "I want to be kind. And sensitive." My voice slowed, as though Gerrick had asked the most serious question of my life so far. Perhaps it *was*.

When I was sixteen, a career advisor at school asked me a similar question. With complete sincerity I told her I wanted to be an actor. "There are jobs on offer at the local steelworks," was her response. She didn't look at me, she just shuffled papers around, choosing one and holding her pencil over a little box on it where a tick mark should go. "They are holding interviews next Tuesday," she continued. "You'll be able to take the afternoon off." Did she believe this was a seductive incentive? To my left another student was agreeing to Tuesday, nodding like an imbecile. I scrunched my nose and pulled my lips to one side.

If the career advisor had looked up at me she might have thought I was considering the pros and cons of going myself on Tuesday, or if Wednesday would suit my busy busy busy sixteen-year-old schedule better. In reality I was thinking, *How could she leave her house this morning wearing that color lipstick?* Evidently my gay gene was already beginning to dominate my sicklier heterosexual ones. Further proof, perhaps, was that I *knew* the black lipstick I was wearing that day was obviously much more sensible. It matched everything. As luck would have it my school uniform, a thrift-store-bought drainpipe-leg suit, was also black. Together with my two-foot-long, equally black spiky hair and my Winklepicker boots, I felt as though I wasn't betraying my truer weekend identity, while at the same time conforming to the school uniform.

Everybody in Accrington, the small industrial town where I grew up, thought I was a freak, but my mum had brought me up Christian so I'd learned to turn the other cheek and be tolerant of others. As far as I was concerned this unhelpful career advisor could dress however she liked and wear whatever lipstick took her fancy. But, style aside, wouldn't you think to check your teeth in a mirror after eating spinach at lunch? The only response I could muster, the one I thought appropriate, was to shake my head and tell her I'd probably work with my father on a building site. "Good, good," she said. Having dealt with me to her satisfaction, she moved the piece of paper with the plans for my life to the bottom of the pile and called for the next child.

Now, as a twenty-three-year-old adult with Gerrick, undoubtedly I knew a lot more about life than I had seven years ago.

So what did I want to be? With some hesitation I said, "I want to be somebody who has a boyfriend." I qualified this three times. "In a loving relationship. With somebody I love. Who loves me." I added the last two points as though they were separate notions that could not necessarily be taken for granted based on simply having a boyfriend.

"Go on," Gerrick said. He leaned forward in his chair, resting his elbows on his knees and clasping his hands, looking as though he thought I was saying something important. "That's three," he continued. "Give me ten."

"I want to live in the country. Is it okay that these aren't jobs?"

"It's your life, Aiden. You write the script."

Something came to me that felt more urgent than my previous answers.

"I'd like my work to involve being creative."

Gerrick smiled, maybe because he could relate to it, or because he knew this kind of work was tough to get. Maybe he just felt self-satisfied that I wanted to be something he already was. Regardless, to me a smile was better than a frown.

"That's five. Keep going, Aiden. Usually the first step to getting anything we want is knowing what it is."

"I guess I'd be lying if I didn't say I'd like to have enough money to be comfortable."

"That's not unreasonable."

By now my hands were sweating. I wiped them on my handkerchief.

"I like a man who uses a handkerchief," Gerrick said kindly, putting me at ease. "It's better for the environment, you know."

"I hadn't thought about it," I said, thinking it a funny concern. "I just like them. They don't fall apart all the time."

"Hey! More answers."

"I want to be funny, and liked."

"You've already nailed those two."

I played with my fingers. "I know this sounds heavy and possibly a bit egotistical, but I'd like to have an effect in the world, to change things, like people's sense of morality, intolerance of gays, of sex workers, of anybody who doesn't necessarily fit the mold. Who made that goddamned mold, anyway?"

"That's so huge we can count that as two if you like."

My head was down. What a moment ago had been teen angst and fight flipped into sadness at how much the world didn't fit me.

"Hey, Aiden." Gerrick held his hand under my chin and lifted my head. My eyes were wet. "Cheer up, sweet man. Those are all achievable things."

"Do you think? I feel like I'm so far away from all of them."

"Then let's get the ball rolling. Do you have any writing I can read?"

"A film script."

"Great."

"I'd save comments like that until you've read it. I doubt it's great. It's called *Would You Adam and Eve It?*"

"I'm guessing that means something I'm not getting."

"It's Cockney slang for *Would you believe it?*"

"Because?"

"It's my interpretation of Genesis."

"That's a mighty big topic to tackle."

"It's not that serious. I'm just fucking with interpretation."

"I get it. Showing that the Bible itself is perhaps interpretation, right?"

"Actually I think parts of it are just common sense, but a lot of it is absolutely absurd. I'm guessing stuff got lost in translation. I like some of the imagery. How I see it my head, anyway."

Gerrick raised his eyebrows. "Will you let me read it?"

I paused. "Yeah. Why not?"

He put the tips of his fingers together and placed them against his lips. "How about this," he said. "What are you doing tomorrow?"

"I'm busy until six but so far I've no plans after that."

"Why don't you drop by with your script and I'll take a read through it."

I paused, unsure. "Err . . ."

"Don't worry, I'll pay you." He gestured to the remnants of food. "Have you had enough of these?"

I nodded.

"Because I have a meeting now." He wheeled towards the door. "Until tomorrow, then?"

"Thank you," I said. I looked at my watch. "I've been here less than an hour."

"That's okay. I'll see you tomorrow, and hopefully I'll learn a little more about you then."

He opened the door, revealing an immaculately dressed woman who obviously was just about to knock. What a vision! My head jerked back. Before me stood the personification of all the most glamorous women ever, with David Bowie from the Ziggy Stardust era thrown into the mix. Her face was architectural, all angles and perfect lines, but at the same time had the poreless, perfect softness of a Michelangelo marble sculpture. She was a hybrid of all modern proportions and fashions, from Mondrian and Rothko to Gucci and Vivian Westwood. I looked at her, enthralled. Even though she was wearing mirror glasses, I could tell she was watching me. Fuck, she was amazing. I could have bowed before her.

Gerrick broke the spell.

"Minty! Come in, come in. Aiden was just leaving." With hurried formality, he added, "Sorry. How rude of me. Minty, Aiden Shaw. Aiden Shaw, Minty."

She raised her head slightly, like people do when blowing smoke out of their mouths. Her acknowledgment made, she stepped in front of me and proceeded into the room. Her perfume was musky and sweet. In that moment I loved her, not the E, chemical kind of love I was familiar with but a kind of love I knew nothing about.

Was that all the information I was going to get about her? Who was she? What was she doing there? Had she come for a film or advertisement casting? She was too cool and stylish to be Gerrick's secretary, too sophisticated to be a hooker, and far too beautiful to be his wife, no matter how wealthy or successful he might be. The Americans I knew usually introduced people by both their first and last names, but she was simply Minty. She must be famous.

I was in the hallway, facing Gerrick.

"Does six-thirty, sevenish sound good?" I said.

"Excellent. I'll be here waiting. Don't let me down."

"See you then."

He shut the door, shifting out of sight as it closed between us. No more Gerrick. More importantly, no more mysterious Minty. I walked down the hallway feeling good about myself and a little confused. At the end of the passage I turned to the elevator. The button glowed, waiting to be pushed. I pressed it. The door opened. I stepped in and was immersed in Minty's scent. The memory of her image lingered as I descended and, somewhat out of it, walked through the lobby and made eye contact with the concierge.

It felt very different from on the way in.

— **6** —

Scavengers, dregs, runaways, the dispossessed, rentboys, punters—these were the patrons of the Golden Lion in Soho. There were two gay pubs, the Brief Encounter and the Compton Arms, but sometimes I preferred to be around broken old queers and the parasites that preyed on them. This was a place where I was comfortable. I fitted in.

Most proper gays wouldn't go to the Golden Lion, so it seemed like an ideal place to meet Love. I didn't want to bump into anyone I knew, because I wanted to give him my full attention and have him all to myself. It had an upstairs area where, midweek at least, you could usually find a place to sit down and they left the windows open so that it wasn't so smoky. Also, being from California, I thought it might interest Love culturally. The place could be a bit daunting if you weren't familiar with it, so I arrived about ten minutes early to secure seats, get him a drink, and welcome him when he came in.

At the bar I squeezed in beside a homeless Mohawk I knew vaguely, who was working a red-faced and bloated punter known as King Charles. I'd watched Charles before and knew his routine. It was impossible to get cash out of him, although he would happily pay for drinks for as long as you spoke to him. The boys used him to get a bit drunk, then worked the pub for other, more giving "cash points," as they called the punters. I ordered a diet cola for Love and a pint of Guinness for myself, with a large vodka chaser, and downed the vodka in one, hoping it would relax me. Love's good looks intimidated me. I found a snug corner upstairs, got out my book, and tried to read, but soon realized how stupid it was to attempt this in a pub.

Fortunately Love was early. In such surroundings he had the look of a brand-new Ferrari in a scrap yard, not the kind of thing I'd normally go for but he wore it well. Desire instantly outweighed my insecurities. After working as a rentboy for so many years, it was surprising that testosterone still rose to the occasion enough to influence my judgment. The welcome I gave Love was warm, masculine. Americans seemed to like my Englishness, so I used words like *mate* and *cheers*. He was charmed that I had a drink waiting for him.

I sipped my Guinness. Love fiddled with his glass. The bar was noisy enough, but the worst thing was a new song called "Like a Prayer" that repeated and repeated on the jukebox.

Finally Love said, "This song is awesome!"

"I figured," I said. "You've mouthed every word, each time it plays."

"Don't you like Madonna? I'm a big fan."

My date's sex appeal instantly dropped.

"I'm not fussed either way," I said. "But I'm surprised she's still popular."

"I think she's going to be huge."

"It's hard to keep the weight off as you get older."

We fell silent again. The noise around us emphasized this and made me feel that if I said something it should be important. Naturally everything I'd wanted to say felt important, because it would be about *us* and might lead to a kiss. At this point I didn't give a fuck about full-on sex. I just wanted Love to want me to kiss him. It was such a simple desire, but so complicated to orchestrate.

I shifted in my seat, leaned on one elbow then the other, then sat back so he could see my crotch, all the while looking for a pose that might make the kiss happen. I knew one thing for sure: Madonna wasn't going to get in the way. Luckily my vodka had begun to affect me, and my confidence expanded.

"Apparently Madonna thinks you're hot shit," I said.

"Stop it!" he said, softening.

"Love, Love, Love, Love," I said. "You're definitely as advertised." I paused. "No, you're much more."

"You're full of compliments," he said, clearly not minding. It was distracting talking to him, because he was so good to look at. I found myself trying to work out what exactly made his face so appealing, in the same way others have done with Marilyn Monroe and James Dean. Was it the proportions? I stopped being pretentious and marked it down to pheromones.

"But don't you think she's got a great voice?" Love said.

"I think she sounds like a teenage pig."

"That's crazy," he said. "Can I quote you on that?"

"I can't imagine anybody ever being interested in anything I have to say, but go ahead."

"Did you read that somewhere?"

"In a book," I said.

"What was it called?"

"*Life*."

"What page?" He seemed slightly irritated, but at least we were interacting.

"One thousand nine hundred and eighty-nine."

"Nineteen eighty-nine," he said, suppressing a smile. "That was almost funny. Was it a good book?" So he liked our conversation enough to go on talking.

"I'm still reading it. In fact I can't put it down. I read it every day."

"Is it easy to follow?"

"Mostly, although it can be unpredictable. Amazing characters turn up out of nowhere, and occasionally they're too beautiful to be true."

"Oh, yeah," said Love, disarmed. "I'm reading one like that too. I don't want it to end."

"It's okay with this one, because it's actually a prequel. So there's already another that follows."

I watched his lovely Adam's apple rise and fall on his stubbly neck as he drank his diet cola.

"Yeah, but sequels are never as good as the first one."

"Ordinarily that's true," I said, having fun with the metaphor. "But allegedly this one is great."

Love leaned forward as though he was keenly interested in a serious debate.

"Really?" he said.

"Well, no, not really. Actually it's a bit sad."

"What a sweet thing to say."

Damn! Love's statement was even sweeter, and he'd managed to access Little Fella, the part of me that had a soft spot for kind men no matter what they looked like, and that was so seldom evoked in my line of work. Meanwhile my young adult sex drive made my dick throb. Despite Madonna it had been chunky for some time. A trickle of precum dribbled out. I sighed, hoping Love wouldn't misread this and think I was bored.

He still had the glass against his mouth. I watched him. He noticed this and responded with warm, smiling eyes. His lashes were short and thick, neat and well placed. They worked perfectly with the rest of his face.

"Is it me," he said, "or does this place smell of vomit?"

"I smell it, too. Don't you think it adds authenticity?"

"Yeah, real charming."

We fell quiet again, but at least the music had changed. The trouble was Love instantly looked bored. He glanced around the pub, taking in the patrons. Now *I* really wanted Madonna to play again. Where was she when I needed her? If one of her songs played again, at least I could keep watching his lips, even if they were synchronized to her words.

"Some real characters, hey?" I said, trying to both keep the conversation going and show some empathy. "Are you here for work?"

Suddenly he looked more serious. "Yes. I leave tomorrow."

"Early?"

"I have a couple of meetings in the afternoon, then I'm taking the red-eye at eight."

I had nothing to lose, he was leaving the next day anyway. "I don't want to come on too strong, but I wish I'd met you earlier."

"Me, too."

"It doesn't give us much time."

With a sultry, totally convincing expression, he lowered his head and looked up at me through his lashes. "But it does give us *some* time."

"What is it about you, Love? Some things you do and say go straight to my dick."

"Good. That's where I was aiming," he said.

My dick throbbed into a full hard-on. I had to adjust it in my pants. Love noticed. We both laughed.

I let out another, deeper sigh. "Let's blow this joint," I said.

"There's an offer I can't refuse," he said.

The street seemed peaceful after the noise of the pub. It was dark out, and surprisingly quiet. We walked from Soho down through Chinatown, where it got noisier again, the air vibrant and saturated with the area's specific smells. With more gaps than words in our conversation, still the link between us felt physical. Our silence dialogued. I maneuvered us into a crowded walkway with lights strung along the sides. It felt festive, like Christmas but without the imagery. Flattened duck hung in restaurant windows and things glittered in shops. Chinese voices mixed with accents from the Midwest, Manchester, France. We had to dodge meandering tourists looking up, backwards, anywhere other than where they were heading. Every so often Love and I would bump elbows or nudge each other. I found myself placing my hand on the base of his spine, above his bum, to steer him. This made my heart beat faster. Every time we made contact the serotonin level rose in my bloodstream.

Love took my hand and pulled me into an alley. The light from the sidewalk fell away. The world we'd been part of just a moment ago felt dull now, somewhere else. He pushed his crotch against mine. The smell of rotting food added to a sordid feeling, which didn't turn me off. I thought of a British film from the Sixties where a young woman became pregnant after getting fucked down a back alley. Aroused, I grabbed the back of Love's head and kissed him around his forehead, neck, and jaw, moving on to the more sacred eyes and lips. He nuzzled my neck. I smelled the top of his head, inhaling slowly, taking in the musk of his hair and scalp.

I pulled his head up. Our eyes, noses, lips were all in line.

"I've got to fuck you," I said.

"You took your time."

"I was making sure I clinched the deal."

"You had me with 'Afternoon, gents' in the steam room. All you had to say was *I've got to fuck you*, and I'd have lain down for you any which way."

"Good boy. Your hotel?"

"It will be crawling with people from work."

"Then my place it is. Let's get a cab. This is an emergency."
Soon we were heading in my front door.

"Wow!" he said on seeing the decor in my apartment.

"That's nothing," I said, dragging him into my bedroom. I pulled out my dick.

"I see what you mean," he said.

"I'm not going to beg you to suck this, but I will if I have to."

"I'm on it, stud."

Love knelt, his head at my hips, his pretty lips on my dick. It flashed into my mind that I liked his mouth doing this more than his mouthing Madonna songs. His hair looked golden in the light from my bedside lamp. As he sucked, his T-shirt came out of his jeans. Bobbing back from my dick for a beat, he managed to pull the shirt over his head and off in one smooth motion and throw it so it landed on my bed behind him—without ever taking his eyes off my crotch.

"You like that, don't you?" he said, noting my excitement. Maybe he did voiceovers for porn movies.

Feeling self-conscious, I attempted a macho reply. "Treat it good and you'll get it good."

"Do you know what's good for me?" he said, looking up, his mouth full of dick. I thought of a ventriloquist but luckily the image didn't stick.

"Of course I know what's good for you," I said, tousling his hair.

"Will I get it?"

If you're not careful, I thought. But I said, "*I'll* get what *I* want, and I'm guessing that's the same thing."

At that moment what I wanted was to merge with him—his cum, his piss, even his blood. This urge took me over completely. I held him by his head, to stop his sucking, and pushed his face around my balls, knocking the side of his jaw with the shaft of my dick then putting it sideways through his lips.

"Shall I be real noisy?" he said, sounding a bit stagy.

"Quiet or loud, just make me believe it."

"Do you think I'd lie?"

Shut up, I thought. "You wouldn't dare," I said.

His eyebrows rose and his mouth formed a huge, helpless grin. I nudged his head backwards with my hips so that he was lying on the bed. I lifted his legs, pulled his trousers round his ankles, and stuck the head of my dick against his butt crack.

He wriggled. "Eat it! Eat it! Eat it!" he said.

Used in this context, *eat* always made me squirm. I couldn't help thinking of shit. Still, Love was so sexy I let go of the idea and put it down to him being American, fixing my mind on the action, not the words. I wasn't in the mood to talk, and it seemed the perfect thing to do with my mouth. Also it was one of my favorite things in the whole world. We could have been anyplace, for all the attention I was able to give to anything beyond us, and more importantly this one specific area.

"Spit on my butt, fucker man!"

It sounded like he had a porn star somewhere deep inside him. Regardless, it seemed polite to do as he'd said.

"Put your dick against my hole." Even though the expression sounded well-used, it made such sense, so when he said, "Now stick it in, daddy boy. Fuck me!" I did. His request to "Plough me good with that uncut dick!" seemed entirely reasonable. And when, after about ten intense minutes, he shouted, "Cum up my butt, you fucking stud!" it seemed the polite thing to do.

A moment later we pulled apart. "You know what I like about you, Aiden?"

"My curly, fluorescent teeth?"

"Goofball. It's that you're such a *guy*. There's not an ounce of woman in you. No camp. Nothing gay, really."

"There's just been some gay in you," I said.

"Some? A lot!"

"It's all I had."

"Stop with the joking. I'm just trying to say that you're very masculine."

"Fooled you, huh? It's all studied."

"Right. You must have gone to some top-notch school then, because you learned so well."

"I'm self-taught."

"What do you mean?"

"I didn't just become a man, it was a decision."

"Whatever. I figure you know what you're going on about, but I've got my opinion *and* I've just had some mighty fine proof."

"Okay. It's not important."

We lay beside each other breathing deeply, satisfied.

"You haven't got AIDS, have you?" he said abruptly.

"No! Do you?"

"No."

"Have you been tested?"

"What are you implying?"

"Nothing. I just wondered if it was different in America."

"What do you mean?"

"You guys have more of it there, don't you?"

He laughed. "You're joking."

"No," I said. "We're told we should be more careful with Americans."

"What garbage."

"Sorry. I don't know that much about it."

"It seems nobody does." He closed his eyes. "Have *you* been tested?"

"Sure!"

"When?" he said.

"A few years ago."

"Technically you could have it."

"Wouldn't I know?" I said. "I'd be dying or something, wouldn't I?"

"Right." He looked happier. "No one in my group of friends has it."

"Good," I said, thinking Love looked too fit to have AIDS.

"I've heard only bottoms get it."

"Really?"

"I'm not a bottom, so I should be clean."

I stroked his hair. "I'm glad you bottomed for me."

"And I never use poppers." He stretched out the word *never* like a drag queen.

"Meaning?"

"God, you Brits are behind. There's a connection. Poppers give you sores all over your body."

"I didn't know."

"Do you still use them?"

He looked concerned. I'd seen old women with the same expression. Where had my golden-haired god gone, my can't-keep-my-hands-off-him, got-to-kiss-him idol? He'd been in the cab with me, and surely I'd spotted him briefly while we were fucking, despite his nonstop narration.

"Poppers? Not really," I lied.

"Actually," Love said, "they say it's about the way gay people live their lives."

"What do you mean?"

"You can only abuse your body so much. There's so many things you can catch, like clap and syphilis and other germs. Your body just gives up." He was on a roll now, looking smug and know-it-all. "When you think of the drugs and crap some of these queens put in their bodies, it's hardly surprising they get sick."

"It's good to know some facts," I said.

"My friends talk about it all the time. These days you've got to know your shit. Your life depends on it."

I took my hand off Love's head. He'd got me thinking, but not in any way I wanted after having sex. He lay at a forty-five-degree angle with his head on my chest. We stared at the ceiling. The conversation had stopped. I think neither one of us wanted to ruin the moment.

The trouble was, any desire I'd felt was gone. I couldn't decide whether it was the topic or the way Love expressed himself—or simply that I'd cum. But I was sure of one thing: I never wanted to see or speak to Love again.

— **7** —

"Is he in there?" one of the five colossal firemen asked me in a clear, profound, altogether perfect voice.

"I think I heard him."

"What's his name?" His words resonated inside me.

"Terry."

Perfect Voice looked at me in a way I didn't understand. Did the name mean something to him? He smiled, then put his face close to the door and spoke through the side of his mouth.

"Terry!"

One of the other five firemen stepped between us and pounded on the door. He had red hair and vivid green eyes. I thought of the children's rhyme "Red and green are seldom seen except upon a king and queen."

"Terry!" he shouted. "It's the fire brigade."

Funny that he referred to himself with his job title rather than as a person.

"Let me," I said, moving between them and crouching down. Opening the letter box, I shouted Terry's name and banged really hard. "It's Aiden." I waited and listened, my ear and mouth taking turns at the letter box. "Say something," I pleaded. "Anything! Just make a noise!"

Although I was concerned about Terry I couldn't help being aware that I had moved into the personal space of these two glamorous men and that I was at crotch level to both of them. They wouldn't have looked out of place in a Hollywood film, whereas their actual backdrop was the graffitied squalor of Terry's council block, smeared with shit, dried vomit, empty cider bottles, and an auburn wig nailed to a pale blue wall. It was five AM. They'd come in response to my urgent call, after I'd been summoned by Terry.

"Anything?" said a fireman with a shaved head who looked like he'd been in too many boxing matches where he'd not done so well. He fidgeted, his broken face twitching.

"Terry!" I shouted again. "Make a noise, baby! Please! It's Aiden." I paused, then shouted even louder. "Terry!" My voice sounded angry. In reality I felt nervous and worried.

A barely audible rasping came from inside the flat.

"Did you hear that? It's him!" I said.

"I did," said Perfect Voice. "Let's get this door off, lads."

Shouts, orders, actions. These men seemed even larger than before, and moved more quickly. My brain blurred. I couldn't keep up with who did what. They repositioned, as calculated and precise as clockworks but more dynamic. My thoughts were jumbled. I couldn't tell if I was noticing things as they happened or remembering what I'd seen afterwards.

Now they were all inside. Lights were turned on. I heard bodies rushing, radio sounds, orders being shouted. Torches flashing, they surrounded the bed. I couldn't see anything but their backs. Suddenly I was a boy, watching soldiers in the movie *Planet of the Apes*. I stood at the doorway, unnecessary, a bystander stunned into stillness.

Terry's sweet, milky smell drifted up my nose, shocking me alert.

My eyes flicked around the room. The first thing I noticed was the depressing view from the window on my right: a scatter of lights from neighboring council flats. This wasn't what I was searching for. Fresh-looking floral curtains framed the window. That meant something. My eyes swept past the firemen to an open drawer with neatly folded T-shirts and underpants. On top of the TV was a framed photograph of Terry as a teenager, standing on a diving board in bright blue Speedos with a medal around his neck and the same little red nose that looked like he'd been kissing for hours, the same sleepy eyes I'd gazed into on ecstasy. And something I'd never seen before. He looked happy.

Carpet, sideboards, a gilt-framed mirror—everything was spotless. This wasn't the labor of the reckless boy I knew. Maybe Terry had a cleaner. But he didn't earn enough to afford one. He must have a sugar daddy. Why hadn't I thought of it sooner? So many men would want to look after him. My eyes fell to the coffee table on my left, to a sheet of pretty primrose-color paper. I read the note:

> *happy 21 birthday !!!!*
> *your the man of the family now*
> *MY SOLDEIR!*
> *see you on monday at 8*
> *luv*
> *mom*
> *xxx*

Emotion swept over me as the real story fell into place. Everything I'd seen wasn't the result of a cleaner paid for by some sugar daddy but the attention of Terry's devoted mother. Today was Monday. Why hadn't he told me it was his birthday?

Beside the note was a bag of coke. Shit! Not wanting to attract attention, I moved towards the bag slowly and managed to put it in my pocket without anybody noticing.

"Can you hear me, Terry?" said Perfect Voice. My attention snapped back. Perfect Voice looked at me. "Did he say what he's taken?" Again he had an expression on his face that I didn't understand.

I stepped towards him.

"Stay back!" ordered Vivid Eyes.

His commanding tone startled me, made me more conscious of the coke in my pocket. This situation wasn't in any way normal for me, but something else confused me. It felt like it had more to do with the firemen themselves.

Perfect Voice spoke again, with more urgency. "Did he say what he's taken?"

I love you, I thought inappropriately. "No," I said. I was upset for Terry but I felt desire for some of the firemen. This random combination was bound to be the result of too many drugs mixed with my raging hormones. And perhaps it had something to do with the fact that I spent so much of my time looking at and fiddling with men I found grotesque, for money.

They returned their attention to Terry.

"Is he okay?" I said to their backs.

"They know what they're doing," said Vivid Eyes, approaching me.

"He likes his coke," I said, feeling completely superfluous. "Downers, too."

"Anything you can tell us helps," said Perfect Voice kindly.

Vivid Eyes sighed.

Broken Face held up an empty bottle. "Temazepam," he read.

He squinted. "Thirty milligrams. It's empty. Hang on a second. Yep, it's a new prescription. Seven days old."

"Cheers," said a man with blond cropped hair and seemingly no emotion who until now had been playing a bit part. "How many were in it?"

"Twenty-eight."

With so much going on I hadn't noticed of the Blond. This was an all-star cast. The Blond moved as though he was made of iron and nothing could stop him, placing himself in front of Perfect Voice and taking over. He checked Terry's pulse, lifted back Terry's lovely lids, and shone a small flashlight into his eyes.

"Is he okay?" I said. Apart from Broken Face, my desire now was for any of the men who would save Terry—and be my boyfriend for the rest of my life.

"The ambulance is here," said Vivid Eyes.

The Blond continued his inspection. "Let's get him downstairs."

A huge medic, who reminded me of the man on boxes of Scott's Porage Oats, leaned in and effortlessly lifted Terry's floppy body. "Got him," he said.

Don't go, I thought. "Can I come with you?" I said.

"Coming through," said Scott's Porage Man, meaning *Move out of the way*.

"Are you family?" said the Blond as he headed towards the door.

No, I thought. I said, "Yes."

The Blond called my bluff. "What relation?"

"I'm very close."

"Leave them to it," said Perfect Voice, stepping in front of Vivid Eyes and blocking the Blond just enough to let me know they meant I couldn't go with them.

Desperate, I said, "He has no actual family."

"Sorry," said Vivid Eyes.

For some reason it bugged me more, coming from him.

"Don't worry," said Perfect Voice. "He'll probably just sleep it off. At worst he might need his stomach pumped."

"What should I do now?" I said, wanting to be held by whoever was the nearest, even Broken Face.

As they got Terry out of the door, Vivid Eyes hesitated, looking bothered.

"Go on," said Perfect Voice. "I've got this covered."

When we were alone, Perfect Voice turned to me. "You okay?" he said.

"I think so," I said, feeling safe and a little more relaxed. I looked around me. Apart from a messy area around the bed the empty flat was still tidy.

"Don't worry, your friend's in good hands," said Perfect Voice gently.

Tears welled in my eyes. I tried to speak but all that came out was crying noises.

He put his hand on my shoulder reassuringly. "Come on, fella," he said. "He'll be okay."

"How do you know?" I said.

"His pupils were responsive to light. I saw it myself."

"What does that mean?"

"Oxygen was probably still getting to his brain. If it wasn't he might have had brain damage."

"What will happen now?"

"He'll be taken to emergency. They'll keep an eye on him until he wakes up."

"What shall I do?"

"The best thing you can do is get some rest. Go home."

"I can't imagine I'll sleep much."

"Try not to worry."

"That's easier said than done."

"Is he a good friend?" He emphasized the word *good*.

"I like him a lot, if that's what you mean."

"Is he your special friend?"

I realized what he meant now. My mum used the word *special* when referring to my boyfriends.

"He's not my boyfriend, if that's what you mean."

"Sorry to beat around the bush. I didn't want to presume."

"I appreciate your being so cool about it."

"Hey," he said. He paused. "I'm sorry about Jim."

My face was blank.

"The guy with red hair."

"What about him?"

"He was a bit rude, shouting at you."

"He was just doing his job."

"I think he noticed me looking at you."

"Why would he care?"

"He's got a crush on me."

"You're joking."

He shook his head.

"And you don't feel the same about him?"

"No. I'm not gay."

I stared out the window, then back at Perfect Voice. "So why were you looking at me?"

"How can I explain?" he said, clearly embarrassed. "I like to look at men and I can tell if they're sexy or not. But it's not sexual."

"That's cool. Unfortunate for me but . . . do you have a girlfriend?"

"No."

"Are you sure you're not gay?"

"I have an eight-year-old son, if that means anything."

"It means you had sex with a woman at least once."

"It's the only proof I have."

"You don't need proof. Anyway, how can I find out if Terry's okay?"

"Call the hospital when you wake up."

"Which hospital?"

"Westminster."

"What about Terry's door?"

"The police will secure it. I'll wait till they get here."

I remembered the coke in my pocket. "I'll leave you to it then," I said, extending my hand. "Thanks for helping Terry."

"It's my job."

"In that case, good job, mate. Jesus, I don't know your name."

"The name's Terry, too."

He shook my hand. The top of his little finger was missing. I flinched, then carried on as though I hadn't noticed.

"I know it can be a bit of a surprise," he said. "Don't let it freak you out."

"It doesn't. How did it happen?"

"On the job."

"You act like it was nothing."

"I can't say I miss it or anything."

"It must be funny, seeing people's responses."

"It is, actually."

I paused. He looked like he was waiting for me to speak.

"I must have a thing for Terrys," I said.

He blushed.

"Are you all so adorable?" I asked.

"You tell me," he joked.

I headed towards the doorway and stopped. "See you later," I said, wishing it were true.

It felt odd leaving him in my Terry's flat, and it had some-thing to do with jealousy. I couldn't explain or rationalize my feel-ings, and certainly I couldn't justify them. All I could do was notice them. I consoled myself by thinking that being aware of these things was at least a start towards one day possibly under-standing them.

In the cab home I stared out the window and watched the city lights go off as the sun rose. I thought of Terry floppy in the arms of the Scott's Porage Man. The Thames looked brown and cold and still. I thought of Terry in the toilet cubicle at Heaven.

Back in Kennington I couldn't get Terry out of my head—his soft, sticking-up, caramel-color hair, his even softer pale skin, his cheeky-looking red nose. To comfort myself I took a warm bath. While I was lying in the water Terry came to mind again—his newborn look that made me want to hold him, take care of him, and fuck him. What happened after he left for work this morning? Had I done something wrong? Could I have done any-thing to make him feel better?

I knew I wasn't going to get much sleep. I also knew I'd be making okay money with Gerrick later. I called the Burlington and left a message on the answering machine saying I couldn't sleep, felt rotten, and wouldn't be in for my next shift. They'd probably believe me. It wasn't a weekend night, so I was unlikely to be partying.

I lifted a thick blanket onto the hooks I'd installed above my bedroom window, to keep the dawn light from coming through, then got into bed and sucked on Jaffa Cake biscuits. Even though it was summer I behaved as though it was cold out, arranging soft, cozy things around me. Hoping it would distract me from tor-menting myself about Terry, I settled in with *Siddhartha*, the book S had given me.

It was daylight outside when I finished reading. I brushed my teeth, turned off my bedside light, and got under my covers, then thought to call Westminster Hospital and ask about Terry.

The telephone was in the living room. Just as I reached for the receiver, it rang.

Tuesday

ONLY A PUNTER WOULD CALL AT SEVEN IN THE morning. After the dimness of the bedroom, the sunlight in the living room seemed bright and made me squint. I answered with my low-pitched-horny-escort voice.

"Hello."

The response was covert, leery, clipped. "Right."

"Who's that?" I said.

"Are you available?"

"Yes," I said, without thinking of the time, my mental state, or the inconvenience.

"Good. Do you do role play?"

"Sure," I said, not having a clear idea of what it meant.

"You do bondage?"

"Of course," I said again, equally clueless.

"You dominant?"

I took this to mean I had to boss him around. "Yeah."

"Have you got a pencil for the address?"

"One second." I reached for the pen and pad I kept near the phone for this purpose.

"Oh, and how much do you charge?"

"What exactly do you want?"

"That's up to you, isn't it?"

Our relationship had already begun.

"You're not just some wanker who wants to play at stuff he doesn't know about?"

"I'm the real thing."

Yikes. "Well then, we'll see what you can handle."

"You sound like the right man for the job." He seemed more satisfied already.

"You're lucky you called *me*. I'm not some kid who doesn't have a clue what they're doing."

"Good. The address is 22 Barrow Road, Hampstead. Basement flat,"

The other side of London. "Got it," I said. "That'll be two hundred pounds plus the cab fare."

"Very well," he said. "I'll leave the front door unlocked. Just push it open and come in. The cash will be on the sideboard. Do you know where I'll be?"

With any luck, on the tube to work, I thought. "You'd better be on the bed, ready," I said.

"Don't worry, I'll be there facedown. Does that turn you on?"

"Just how I like 'em. Bum ready for action." *Oh, well,* I thought, *another freak, another dollar.*

"I'm really looking forward to this," he said.

"Me, too."

"Very good, sir."

"What's your name?"

"Boy."

This took me a second to understand.

"Excellent. See you soon."

I put on my jeans and a T-shirt. Boy wouldn't be able to see me until I was naked so it didn't matter much what I wore. Ordinarily *naked* would be the appropriate outfit, but I hadn't a clue when it came to role playing. I looked up the punter's address in the A-Z street map of London to make sure it was real. Terry flashed into my head again. This time he was smiling because I'd said something cheesy. I called Westminster Hospital.

"I'm calling to find out about a friend of mine who was brought to the emergency room earlier," I said urgently, clearly upset.

"First of all, son, slow down," the man who answered said cheerily. His voice instantly made me feel a little better. "I'm putting you through. Hold the line."

This time a female voice answered.

"I'm trying to find out about a friend of mine," I told her. "He'd have been brought in last night. Sorry, it was this morning."

"What's the name?"

"Terry."

"And the surname?"

Damn. "I'm sorry, I've known him ages but I don't know his last name."

"I'm afraid . . ."

"Please, I'm really worried," I blurted out. "He took an overdose and he called me. I had to get the fire brigade to break his door down. It must have been about five, five-thirty."

"Let me see what I can do . . . Does the name Terrence Rutherford sound familiar?"

I recalled seeing it on a bank card when chopping coke. "That's him."

"Hold the line."

While I waited I struggled to dress, cradling the receiver between my ear and my shoulder. The last item of clothing I put on was my jacket. I felt the bag of coke in the pocket.

"Hello?" the woman's voice came again. "Don't worry. Your

friend's fine. He's sleeping at the moment. It's probably best to call back in a few hours and ask for the admissions ward. Be sure to remember the surname—and don't you go telling anyone I told you."

"Thank you *so* much!" I said.

I put my trainers on and snorted two lines of Terry's coke, then went into the bathroom to brush my teeth and gargle. Back in the living room I grabbed the paper with Boy's address. The coke began to kick in. Now the gray walls around me seemed less dismal, the idea of leaving the security of my flat and entering the bright morning sunlight was less alarming, getting a cab to go all the way across London seemed less arduous, and the prospect of acting the domineering SM master not altogether doomed at the outset.

About fifty minutes later I got out of the cab on Barrow Road, a residential street of white-terraced Georgian houses, and headed down a flight of stairs to the basement flat of number 22. The front door was ajar. As I entered, a muffled voice came from one of the rooms. (There were two closed doors, so it could have come from either.)

"Help yourself to a drink. There's sherry on the side. If you want something stronger, there's port in the cupboard above the kettle. The kitchen's straight ahead of you."

"Cheers," I shouted back.

"But don't close the front door. Leave it as you found it. Don't worry, the cat won't get out. She's in the cellar, she's just had a litter."

"Okay," I said. Although the cellar sounded spooky it didn't concern me that Boy wanted the door left open. I'd have a clear escape route.

I poured a tumbler of sherry, took a banana from the bowl of fruit in the kitchen, and headed back towards the voice. As I opened the first door a near-overpowering smell hit me, an odd mix of furniture polish and lavender oil. The room's decor reminded me of the houses my father took me to when I was a boy, after Mass on Sundays when we visited elderly women. The wallpaper had an intricate park scene of people boating, having picnics, and women strolling with parasols. Every piece of furniture was hardwood, with porcelain dolls everywhere, each figure hand-painted in fine detail and all of them in costumes. I'd seen similar "collectors items" in American infomercials. One of the chairs had a cro-cheted blanket thrown over the back. Beside it was a tray on which sat a Willow Pattern china teapot and cup and a mismatched saucer with a half-eaten piece of shortbread biscuit on it.

All this took seconds to register. I barely stopped before moving on to the next room, where quite a sight awaited me: an old man, naked, lying facedown in bed. He'd been tied up with cord and had a black plastic garbage bag over his head. Somebody else must have been there before me to prepare him.

"What have we here?" I said, using my police constable voice. "Very nice!" As I spoke, I checked out the room to make sure it was safe.

Carefully laid out on the bedside table were six evenly cut pieces of cord. Lined up beside them were six wooden rods with smooth, rounded ends. Next to these was a folded red handker-chief. These looked as though they belonged in a kindergarten, but not the five bottles of poppers behind them. Why so many, I wondered. Everybody I could think of had only two nostrils.

"What a treat!" I said. In an attempt to get Boy excited, I spoke slowly, as if I were in a horror film, using my theater training to make it sound as though I'd just come across some-thing precious. "What can I say?" (*Disgusting? What am I doing here? Are you for real?* came to mind but remained unspoken.) Standing next to his bagged head, I whispered menacingly, "I'm gonna make you wish you'd never been born!"

With my half-eaten banana in one hand, I prodded his bum cheek with the forefinger of the other. His clammy silver-salmon skin responded as though submerged in deep water. The impression from my finger lingered.

"Get . . . fucking . . . ready!" I said, having no idea what I was going to do to follow up such a bold statement.

I heard the front door shut. My stomach jumped. Was it the police? I panicked, trying to reassure myself that I was doing nothing illegal. What could be more normal than hanging out in a room with a naked old man? But he was tied up, which might look like I'd kidnapped him.

I moved away from the bed, reached for the cash on the sideboard, and pushed it down behind it, hiding the evidence. I tried to control my erratic breathing. At least I wasn't undressed. But maybe my being dressed with him naked on the bed would look more incriminating.

Banana in hand I sat down on a green leather chair, trying to appear nonchalant. Perhaps if I spoke to Boy as though we were old friends and he just happened to be tied up with a garbage bag over his head . . .

"Expecting company?" I said.

Luckily he wasn't gagged. If necessary he could explain this dubious-looking situation to our visitors—unless it was a setup. I took deep breaths, trying to act as though I was breathing normally.

"We're in here," said Boy to whoever was in the hall.

A deep voice responded. "Okay."

My fantasy of a perfect man appeared in the doorway. He looked Middle-Eastern: hairy, dark, and stubbly. He glanced briefly at me, smiling. I felt butterflies in my stomach. I followed his eyes to the banana in my hand and sheepishly ate the last of it.

"How you doing, Boy?" he said.

As he entered the room he pulled his T-shirt over his head. I looked on in awe. Kicking off his trainers, he flicked open the button of his faded jeans. They dropped around his knees. He hooked the sides of his red briefs with his thumbs and slid them down. He was stunning. He pulled the jeans and underpants off, walked over to the bed, and knelt beside Boy, gesturing me to join him, then tugged on the pocket of my jeans, which I took to mean *Take these off*. There was nothing I wanted to do more.

I raised my hand to say hello. He nodded, his eyes smiling, an I-could-give-you-every-physical-pleasure-you-could-ever-want smile that made me want to do something for him.

"Can I get you a drink?" I said.

"I know where it is."

He left the room. My eyes followed his hairy bum and his slim but natural-looking physique. By the time he got back I was naked too. We looked at each other—for a moment, forever—two naked strangers, both aroused. I hoped he felt anything near the same way I did.

We knelt on the bed at either side of Boy. Beautiful Stranger was in front of me now, inches away. I stroked the thick black swirls of silken hair on his chest and abdomen with the back of my hand. He put his arm around my waist, drawing me towards him. Boy lay motionless between us. After a moment we pulled apart. We had work to do.

I slapped Boy's bum, and Beautiful Stranger made the appropriate noises. To impress my colleague I pulled Boy's dick and balls from underneath him and tied a piece of cord around it all, fastening it securely. Following the unwritten law that sex workers must not talk to each other, I mouthed the words, "What's your name?"

"Rock's here now, Boy," Beautiful Stranger improvised, winking at me. "You know you're going to get a good seeing to now."

I smiled, feeling coy. Rock spat on his fingers, put them against Boy's bum, and massaged his hole. He looked at me, then at the wooden rods, directing me with his eyes. I picked up one and held it. Rock moved his eyes again. I picked up another rod. A third time he moved his eyes, more slowly. He smiled, raised his eyebrows. Now I had three rods in my hand. He nodded, closed his eyes. Opening them, he flicked his glance to Boy's bum hole.

I followed his instruction.

"Take this, you piece of shit," said Rock, and flicked his head once more.

I pushed the rods tentatively into Boy's hole. They slid in with ease. I continued pushing. When I could hardly keep hold of them Rock took over, pushing them in completely. The rods disappeared from view as Boy's sphincter closed around them. He didn't seem to respond.

Rock took a bottle of poppers from the bedside table, poured some on the red handkerchief, inserted it into the bag on Boy's head, and left it there. Boy moaned, making noises like animals at a feeding trough.

Rock contracted his fingers and thumb and edged them into Boy's bum beside the rods, leaning forward and pressing his other hand firmly on Boy's head. In the process, he almost touched my face. I didn't move, enjoying our nearness. Rock looked at me, knowing exactly what I was doing. Boy couldn't see this intimacy so it didn't feel rude to be interacting this way when our focus should be on him.

Rock turned away from me to look at Boy's bagged head beneath us, and I tipped towards him just a fraction. When he turned back our noses nudged and our lips met. My whole being answered this small action. My dick, until now only plump due to the coke, became hard and vertical. Physically I was lost in the action yet mentally I was full of insecurity, hoping our kiss had as much effect on Rock as it did on me.

Boy noticed the silence. Despite the rods and most of Rock's hand in his bum, having his face mashed into a plastic bag, and being high on poppers, he knew that something wrong was happening, something disgustingly nice, and so he had to stop it. He tried to get up.

"Keep still, cum bucket," I ordered, trying to make it sound as though Boy was of consequence, was still involved, that we were here for him. He was paying, so he had the power.

My pathetic attempt seemed to work. Lost in his own physicality, Boy writhed beneath us as Rock and I returned to our real business, leaning into each other and putting our lips together again. We opened our mouths this time. With one hand I pulled the ball-cord below, balancing myself by holding my other hand on Rock's biceps. Between the two of us we had no more spare limbs. Our shoulders and torsos folded into each other, the only embrace possible for us. We continued to kiss.

It felt so romantic.

Exhausted, I arrived home just after noon. All life had been sucked out of me. Even though I don't believe in the soul, I imagine that what I felt now would be referred to as soulless. One consolation was that memories of Rock left a delicious aftertaste. I thought to have a bath, to soothe myself, but I had no will to attempt it or energy to achieve it. Not that I minded going to sleep with Rock on my skin. As far as Boy was concerned I'd only touched him with my hands and I'd already washed them several times before I left his flat, as much because of his cat as for sticking rods up his arse.

Back in the safety of my home, my first thought was to pop some sleeping tablets in my mouth. All I wanted to do was get undressed with nobody watching, pull on my soft, light-blue pajamas, and put myself to bed. But first I had to brush my teeth.

With little impetus or drive left in me, I had to rely on habit. This *habit* felt hardwired—more insidious than impulse, more tedious than instinct. Even as I went through the actions I pondered its control over me. The sleeping tablets were already working their magic, unfastening my thoughts from reason. I headed to bed. This routine had changed little since I was a boy. If I was too old for a teddy bear, this wasn't the time to mind. Mum had given it to me and between us we'd stuffed it with sentiment. Even in the dark it came easily to hand, immediately reassuring. By the time the tablets hauled me into sleep I felt nothing much at all.

I woke in a pit of fear. My solution wasn't imaginative but it was a sure thing: more sleeping tablets. It seemed sensible to take them before I ate anything, so the digestion of the food wouldn't delay their knocking me out. Having food in my stomach also lessened the chances of me vomiting, choking, and dying in my sleep. With these and more negative thoughts cycling in my head, I remembered my real life. Terry.

I called the hospital. The head nurse on his ward told me he'd already left. His mother had picked him up. Although relieved that he was well enough to leave, I wondered where he'd gone. Not back to his flat with the broken door. I wished I'd known it was his birthday. None of this would have happened if I'd kept him with me. Why hadn't I?

I recoiled further from the day. But before I shut down I called Gerrick. It was already six o'clock.

"Gerrick, I can't come by tonight," I told him.

"No problem, buddy. Let's take a rain check. Maybe tomorrow?"

"I had to go to hospital with a friend last night. Not much sleep."

"You don't need to explain. Get a good night's sleep and call me tomorrow. Hopefully we can get together then. And don't forget to bring your writing."

Gerrick's response cut through my misery. He made me feel the world had some order.

"Okay," I said, cheered a little. "I'll call you tomorrow."

I took my tablets, ate as planned, and headed back to bed and the bittersweet solace of sleep.

Wednesday

— 1 —

THE NEXT TIME I WOKE A NEW DAY HAD ARRIVED, AND with it an impulse to get up. Still, I took it slowly. Coffee in bed was the first step, comfort reading the next. In the past when feeling unsure, reading "The Happy Prince" by Oscar Wilde usually helped. I cried throughout it, and shut the book feeling that at least one person in the world was as soft as me. Now I was able to get out of bed without the intention of scurrying to collect something and get straight back in.

I thought about Terry as I got dressed. It seemed likely that his mum would have taken him to her house to look after him. Considering the circumstances, I'd be surprised if she ever let him out of her sight again. For now I had little option but to try calling him in a few days and see if he was back in his own place yet. If he was, I'd pop around to his flat and try to make him feel nice, appreciated, even loved, within the parameters of which we were capable.

But now I had to get ready for the day ahead, physically and mentally. I got myself together quickly and left the flat, planning to shower at the YMCA after my workout. The tube ride to the gym was bearable, mainly because I kept myself busy by jotting down thoughts about the last few days. The process of writing things down seemed to help me make sense of them. After this weekend I felt like I was on a conveyor belt assembly line. After each massive thing pounded me, another would come my way and pound me again. Each time I was altered, less like the person put onto the belt, and it wasn't as though I could stop the world happening to me. All I could do was hope I ended up the desired shape, a product of some use to somebody, possibly even myself. At that moment I wouldn't have minded stepping off the conveyor belt for a vacation, or at least a tea break. Obviously I'd have to get back on again; it was my life and nobody else could live it for me. Also, I wouldn't wish it on anybody.

When the doors opened at Tottenham Court Road I was lost in thought. I just managed to get out as they began to shut. I stood and watched the train depart, then slowly walked down the platform, past the ticket barriers, and veered towards the exit closest to the YMCA—all without thinking. I'd made this journey at least four times a week for over a year: turn right, cross the little road, left into the building.

The same people checked my pass at reception. Sitting one flight down in the café were some of the same people I saw every time. I could have set my watch by a few of them, if I had a clue how to use it. The watch was digital, a gift from a Chinese punter. I liked that it looked retro and had a raw quality, unlike the new Swatch watches everybody else was wearing. I had another that I kept in a box by my bed with a few things I felt sentimental about, a grandfather's watch I'd found in a Brighton thrift shop a few years ago. The old woman behind the counter had laughed at me, calling it junk, but she still charged me fifty pence for it.

As I continued down the stairs I noticed somebody out of the corner of my eye. It wasn't my style to cruise. Because of my work

I was always tired, so I never had the inclination, and it seemed extravagant to waste an orgasm. Normally I wouldn't turn back. But this time I did.

David was emerging from a balcony area; two steps more and I'd have missed him. Maybe there's a scientific reason for what happened, and I'm certain there are hundreds more mystical ones, but suddenly I knew this was the moment to approach him. He looked so adorable, scrubbed clean, post-workout. I could only assume I looked like the weekend I'd just had. I had yet to shower, so technically some bits of the weekend were actually still on me. Sometimes I felt as though the things I'd experienced in life had, on a profound level, soiled me; at the very least they clung to me or hovered about me like flies. Not wanting to pretend I hadn't turned around to catch him, I kept my eyes on David, waving as I walked up to him, every step self-conscious. I felt like a cartoon figure put together one painstaking frame after the other.

"David," I said. I was still a little too far from him. At the correct distance I said, "I meant what I said on Saturday. In Heaven."

There he went again with that smile of his. It must get him anything he wants.

"But more than that . . ."

I paused. Nervous energy only got me so far. When it came to the real point of my approaching him my thoughts slowed down, my tongue faltered. My mouth stopped working, slightly open. I tried to reboot it with a laugh but it was only from my head and didn't ring true. Still I went on, like something wound up, snapped, and let loose.

"I wondered . . ."

David smiled again, less sparkly, more sincerely. He must have a whole vocabulary of smiles. What he lacked in words he made up for by not walking off.

". . . if you'd go on a date with me. Maybe this weekend? Friday?"

Done. That wasn't so hard.

He didn't reply.

"Or do you already have plans? You don't have a boyfriend, do you?"

These last two questions jangled out of my mouth like spilt pieces of a jigsaw puzzle. All I could do in their wake was laugh, which made David laugh too. By the time we'd recovered, it was as though the date had already been arranged. We'd shared something already. *Us* had begun. All we had to do now was realize it.

"*Yes* to the date," he said, lifting his hair off his forehead. "And *no* about the boyfriend."

"Phew—about both," I said. "I'm sorry, but with all the good intention in the world I don't think I could have asked you out any better."

"I liked it."

"And I like you for liking it, or for lying. At this point I don't have the luxury of minding which. To tell the truth, I want to move straight on to the second date, because I'll be less nervous and you'll already like me, or you wouldn't be there."

David looked puzzled. After a moment he said, "Let's get through Friday first."

"Of course . . . Sure . . . I mean, great!"

By this point I was trying to work out how this had happened. Then I got back to arranging our date.

"Shall we swap numbers?"

I pulled out the pen I'd been using on the tube. The only thing I could find to write on was a cinema stub. I tore it in half. Along with my number I wrote, in tiny letters, "Maybe the most beautiful man I've ever seen."

David took it and squinted to read it. He turned it over to see what the film was.

"*Female Trouble*. What's that?"

"A John Waters movie."

"Was it good?"

"*Bad* would be a better way to describe it, but in the best possible way."

On his piece of stub, even smaller than mine, he simply wrote "David" followed by his number.

"Where do you live?" I said.

"East seventeen."

"Wow. I mean, where's that? What's it called?"

"Walthamstow."

He may as well have just told me the name of a remote Amazonian village. I wondered how to continue the conversation without sounding stupid, insulting him, or both.

"I hear you," said David, sensing my distress. "Where do you live?"

"Kennington." I wanted it to sound equally weird but had no idea how to achieve this.

After a beat he said, "I've heard of it."

It took me a couple of seconds to realize he was joking. "Good one," I said.

His lips moved slightly; probably he was repeating the word Kennington in his head. It seemed a good moment to make my getaway and leave him, if not on a high note, at least not on a low one.

"I'd better go," I said. "I haven't got long before work."

Immediately I wished I hadn't said this. Next would come the inevitable question, *What do you do?*

I waited. David didn't ask.

"Maybe a film?" he said as I picked up my bag and turned to leave. He was holding up the ticket stub with my number on it.

The smile on my face grew. This lovely boy was talking to me about going on a date, and it was making me respond in a normal way. How simple, easy, and natural. Somehow, David had managed to make me feel calm, happy, attractive, and confident. How strange.

I nodded, almost giddy with happiness. This was exactly how Little Fella would have liked to feel all the time, if I let him. Which I didn't. Why? Perhaps I didn't really like him and so fought hard to be something else. Or did I love and care about him so much that I couldn't bear to inhabit him? Surely to have him see, hear, and feel the world would have killed me.

— 2 —

Considering it was so soon after taking drugs, my workout wasn't that bad. Sweaty and smelling ripe, I headed straight to the showers. When the water finally hit my skin it felt so good, cleansing away the evidence of the weekend. The workout hurt a lot and took a lot of mental effort. Thankfully I'd always had will power—and discipline and a curious amount of control over my body. I'd read somewhere that people with anorexia or bulimia feel out of control in life and their reaction is to control their bodies. This made sense to me. Outwardly I appeared fit and healthy but I wondered if my behavior might be an unhealthy reaction to something, even if the control I exerted over my body was useful to me. If I ate carefully and worked out a lot I looked better naked, which in turn resulted in my earning more money. If, however, it was an eating disorder, possibly even a variety of Body Image Distortion Syndrome, I should take it seriously, examine the possible causes, and find out if there was anything I could do about it.

I wasn't about to do any of these things. I was too busy getting mileage out of this control over my body. I was comfortable to let it be, earn a good living, and have fun. If one day in the future I became a lonely, fucked-up halfwit with some chemical dependency, I'd probably throw myself off a tall building or under a train—although in my heart of hearts I couldn't imagine ever becoming such a sad case or having the guts to kill myself. I guess if I took drugs often and intensely enough, eventually it would have the same effect: to slowly but surely kill me.

Washed, dried, and thoroughly cruised, I made my way to the Burlington. On the walk from Tottenham Court Road to Green Park, random but essential thoughts came to mind like: *road, car coming, don't cross, I'm hungry*. At times this process became useless, formless mind mud without focus or purpose. Actual words appeared, sometimes as noise, other times as visuals, vivid and affecting. Recent and distant memories haunted me: the ugly curl of a drag queen's nostril, the lisping side-of-mouth comments at the gym, the hurt in my mum's eyes. Random, clubby gay scene faces terrorized me. Then I'd be annoyed with myself. How could I let myself forget wonderful things like kissing some of the loveliest lips on the planet?

Thankfully David came easily to mind, perhaps because I'd just seen him and he'd had impact. Terry was also in my thoughts, although it was difficult to stay fearful for his well-being without also picturing kissing, cuddling, and fucking him.

Such was the reality of coming down from the weekend of taking drugs.

My intention was to hurry inside and change clothes but when I arrived at the Burlington I discovered that Sleeve had gone on an errand, leaving S to watch the door. Encountering S was like coming upon a five-star hotel in a war zone.

I paused. "Sweetness!" I said.

"Shady!"

S's name for me felt more appropriate than usual this afternoon. As with most things S said or did, it was meant with no malice, agenda, or hidden meaning. S was one of the only people I knew who had mastered the art of always thinking, feeling, and meaning nice things.

To avoid Sandy I literally got down on my knees and crept quietly below the reception desk. I changed my clothes quickly. If only it were as easy to change other things about me. Unfortunately I was stuck with my outlook on life, my doubts, and my general mood. Once in my uniform I went back to the front desk and asked Sandy why I didn't have any bookings. In his thick, camp, grating Welsh accent, he told me that he hadn't realized I'd arrived. After a few minutes I let on that I'd crept in.

To my surprise, he laughed. Even more shocking, he let a residue of good humor linger on his face. Until now I hadn't been aware that he could show this range of expressions, let alone hold them for seconds. Seeing him smile gave me a nice feeling in my tummy. I made a mental note to make him smile more often.

Myles, a club member, came walking towards reception. I call him a club member because he wasn't really a punter. I don't know if he even used the steam room or sauna. My understanding was that he simply liked to work out in a gay environment. (I'd heard that there were gay gyms in LA, San Francisco, and New York. This was reason enough to want to go to these places. The thought of American men in gyms being available for sex was as much as my young heart desired. In London gyms you found only a smattering of gays, the YMCA having more than others.) No doubt part of Myles's reason for joining the Burlington was that it allowed him to work out without a T-shirt. Also, Myles dated the boys and there was always a steady turnover. He had a good, well-paid job high up in the largest national children's charity. His car was flashy. He was easy to have around. More valuable than his trappings was Myles's good heart. He was generous, considerate, and cared about people. Currently he cared about Cubus, and because Cubus and I were friends Myles had little choice but to care about me, too.

"Mr. Shaw!" This was the greeting he always gave me, along with a big, carefully considered if not tactical smile.

Myles was sweating, I guessed from working out. Once he'd achieved his pump-and-glow he generally strutted around the club to show it off. There were several reasons why I didn't mind him doing things like this. The most obvious was that I felt sorry for him, not because he was balding and wore his white sweatpants high on his waist to cover his love handles, or that the proportions this gave his body were like a toddler's and he never dated anybody less than twenty years younger than him. Ultimately the thing that made me feel a pang for Myles was that he was inherently hobbit-like. My guess was that this stemmed from his growing up at a time when it was much more difficult to be gay. I wouldn't have been surprised if he was called names like *fairy* or *fatty*. Underneath his strutting and bravado I sensed profound meekness and sadness.

Although Myles behaved as though generally he would do whatever the boys wanted, my understanding was that he never really let go of the helm. He managed this simply by having a car. A set of wheels goes a long way for getting to and from clubs, picking boys up and dropping us off if he wanted to see us, and even for the occasional trip out of town when he wanted us away from the distractions of the city and competition. A car meant freedom, and ultimately this was what Burlington boys were desperate to have—freedom to buy clothes, take lots of drugs, fly abroad, and pay extravagant rents. None of us could afford these things without working at the Burlington. Many of us wanted something more fundamental: freedom from "normal" life.

Either we were inherently different, possibly on a cellular level, and couldn't relate to *normal*, or our notion of normal had been played or fucked with along the way. Whatever the reasons, *normal* didn't fit us and we didn't fit it. We had few options—and we would do virtually anything to obtain freedom from it.

"Hello, Myles," I said. "Is Cubus here?"

"He starts at six."

Sandy, his manner still light and joking, said, "Ten pounds says it'll be more like half-past six."

"I don't fancy them odds," I said with a wink, colluding with Sandy. Why not try and keep him in his changed mood? Cubus was none the wiser, and he wouldn't have minded if he knew my motive.

"Aiden," said Myles. "I'd like a quick word."

"Aye-aye, Captain." This expression came to mind easily when I saw Myles—*Captain* because of his ruddy complexion, particularly his red cheeks, and *aye-aye* because it was the name of a nocturnal rodent-like primate in Madagascar. This creature had a round head, large eyes and ears, incisor teeth, and an elongated, twig-like finger on each hand which it used to pry insects from bark. This was something Myles didn't need to know.

Myles led me to a quiet spot in the TV room. "What are you doing for Christmas?" he asked.

"Christmas already? It's not even in the shops yet."

"I know. I'm just trying to plan ahead."

"Sorry, Myles, I really can't say. It's too early. I might be dead by then."

As I turned to leave, I caught sight of the video. Myles followed my eyes. He was always watching what other people—especially his boys—were looking at. I imagine that by doing this he felt privy to what they were thinking. Why he had to know what others thought was not my concern.

"What do you think of that Jeff Stryker guy?" he said.

"I'm not really into porn."

"But what do you think of *him*?"

"It's hard to say. I don't know him. He has a big dick and is pretty vocal, if a bit repetitive."

"Do you find him attractive?"

"Not at all."

Myles persisted. "Why?"

A punter wandered into the video room with an unlit pipe hanging from his drooping bottom lip between two puffy, sagging cheeks, interrupting us. He had one towel tied around his waist and another placed jauntily over his shoulder.

"Afternoon, chaps!"

"Afternoon," I replied. It was my job to be courteous.

I turned back to Myles. "He reminds me of a blow-up doll." Remembering the bulk of the new man in the room, I pointed to the screen. "That porn model. What's with the sudden interest in my taste in porn models?"

"Just wondered."

"Why? What are you up to? I'm sensing a subtext. Are you trying to fix me up with somebody?"

"Silly," he said, shaking his head like a weary schoolteacher late on a Friday afternoon. "It's just that I overheard somebody in the gym who knows somebody in LA that makes videos."

"First, that's a bit tenuous. Second, it's a bit creepy—that you listen in to other people's conversations."

Myles rubbed his temples and sighed, frustrated because our communication wasn't as easy as he wanted it.

"I was thinking of *you*, Aiden."

I looked at him blankly.

"I thought you might be interested. It sounds like easy money."

"Interested in what?"

"Doing a movie."

"You mean shoot one? I haven't done any film work since college."

"Are you trying to be difficult, Aiden?"

"Obviously they're difficult questions, because I'm getting the answers all wrong."

"I meant *be in* one!"

My eyes flicked back to the video. "Are you kidding me?"

The man in the room with us caught my eye. He must have thought I was referring to him, because he scurried out faster than his size and shape ordinarily would have permitted.

On a deeper, barely discernible level, I was excited. "What kind of money were they talking?" I asked Myles.

"I don't know!" he said, annoyed. "They didn't go into their accounts."

This was Myles's idea of being bitchy.

"So how do you know it's easy money?"

"Aiden. You'd be fucking pretty guys instead of the punters here."

Bless him. He knew the slang and he was confident enough to not consider himself one of them. Some boys dated him, but others would have put him in the punter category. To be fair, the only real difference was that instead of cash Myles used props, treats, and making boys' lives easier.

"Get a little real for once in your life, Myles. Do I look like a porn star?"

"With a few tanning sessions, why not?"

"And the stupid way of talking? I can't do that. And how do they manage to be so rigid and fake at the same time? I'm not that good an actor."

Myles held his head in the air. "I quite like it, and I believe I'd be correct in saying it's very popular," he said as though he was standing by his taste in wine.

I shrugged. "Who was it that was talking about it? Anybody I know?"

"That fat redhead."

"The guy who always smells of kebabs? He's so sleazy."

"I guess so."

A pair of punters walked into the video room and stood a foot away from us. Either they had no awareness of personal space or they thought sex was occurring. Without a thought to be cruel or intimidate them, I burst out laughing. It just happened. They meandered out of the room, leaving Myles and me alone with Jeff and his twink co-star.

S joined us. He tapped me on the arm. "You've got a Hillman," he said.

Some of the boys used this expression for a punter. Hillman was Cockney for Hillman Hunter, an early make of car known as a banger.

Myles led the way out of the TV room, a little distraught. He tended to waddle more than walk, at least from the waist down. His feet even turned out like a duck's. He looked like some photograph from the old days of the British Empire. But his upper body was rigid. With his stomach sucked in (rather than tensed), his shoulders placed back, and his lungs filled with air, making his chest jut out, he came across as comical but also endearing. I think I'm safe in assuming that none of this was intended. If only he weren't afraid of turning his image dial down by half, he'd have looked more believable, and he might not have found it all so exacting. It made me giggle to think that, alone at home, he occasionally took the night off and let it all hang out and fall into whatever shape it wanted to.

— **3** —

Sandy gave me the room number and handed me two towels. He still had the vestiges of the good humor I'd procured earlier. The corners of his mouth hoisted up in his version of a smile and he attempted to say something funny. I appreciated his effort. In return, I did an adequate rendition of a laugh, thinking it was okay for me to be false if it made Sandy feel less freakish. This wasn't a selfless act. It was tactical. It did no harm to have the receptionist on your side. Sometimes a new punter didn't ask for anybody by name and would ask Sandy who was *good*.

As I walked down the corridor to massage room three, my comedown hit me hard and mercilessly. *Not now*, I thought. *Not before a punter*. The mirrors lining the hallway flung back my reflection. Countless Aidens lurched up behind me, before me, spooking me from either side. One was usually too much; this was horrible excess. I tried not to notice them. When I finally got to the cunty little room there were only four of me to ignore. I was relieved. This was far from my usual feeling when entering a massage booking—unless a beautiful surprise happened to be waiting for me.

Unfortunately this wasn't one of those occasions. Lying face up on the massage table was a five-foot-long rasher of fried bacon, the sinewy, meatless kind served at diners. Only this one looked as though it had been left in the desert sun for many, many dehydrating years. Unknown to Rasher on the table, I took the psychological equivalent of a deep inhalation of air. I slowly let out my mental breath, releasing it with measured control, hoping for optimum effect. Finally I believed I was ready for any eventuality, while reminding myself that *ready* is not the same as *prepared* or necessarily *able to cope with*.

All this mental preparation lasted as long it took to close the door, stuff a wad of tissue between the door and the frame, and take the first steps towards inducing Rasher to want extras. With calculated casualness I lifted my T-shirt at the front, making sure to tense my abs, then pulled it over my head and tucked it into my shorts. My last ploy was to rearrange my crotch. This part of the show being over, I said to Rasher, "Great tan" (as in *great war* and *great depression*, though I kept this to myself).

He had no towel covering his disproportionately huge dick and balls. This mass of genitalia was much darker than the rest of him. It looked like several pounds of black pudding, to my mind not the kind of thing anyone would want to put in his mouth even if it could possibly fit. It would have been too much for a party of six, unless they were extremely hungry. I had met the odd individual who'd attempt such a feast but I couldn't help thinking that getting full wasn't the real issue, because even when stuffed they'd usually want another helping, plus some kind of tricky dessert.

"I must look horrible to you," said Rasher.

The words tugged at my heart. I couldn't bear hearing a man put himself down, especially when comparing himself to me. It made me feel it was my fault. My automatic reaction was to defend him. I'd already begun to like him. I found a way to validate my feelings.

"Actually, you've a Clint Eastwood look about you," I said.

"Stop it." The way he said this was adorable. He added, "I'm not that old."

"I know," I lied. "But don't you think he's really sexy?"

"Do you think?"

"I'd do him in a heartbeat," I said, "although I'd prefer to take all night, make him breakfast, and never leave his side again. Apart from when he's on set. I wouldn't want to get in the way of his career."

"I'm sensing that you like him."

"You picked up on that?" My balls budged. "Do you mind turning over so I can work on your back?"

He rotated his chin as he turned, facing me as much as he could and giving me the most endearing smile. It must have been uncomfortable for him, but nothing about his expression seemed staged or jaded. A massive surge of sexual desire hit my gut.

"I've trained in Swedish deep tissue massage," I said idiotically. Who cared what qualifications I possessed? This was about me touching him, connecting physically with him. "Sounds sexual, doesn't it?" I added, to put us back on track.

"*Deep* does," he said. "*Tissue* makes me think of nasal passages."

As soon as he was facedown my mission was set in stone. He had the bum of a fourteen-year-old! I'm no expert on teenage bums, but I knew they were higher, plumper, and stuck out more than adults' did. I'm not a pedophile, but this bum was irresistible.

"But I'm happy to go with your idea," he continued, unaware that he was now totally desirable to me.

"Nice bum," I confessed, drawing out both words to show him I meant what I said. My gut was in the driver's seat now and I trusted it as a place of pure, unadulterated honesty. It was also clever. I'd known it to outsmart my brain on many occasions.

"Really?" he said.

The inflection in his voice made me believe he'd never been told this before. (The usual response was *Help yourself*. I'd heard it too many times before.) Maybe he'd never come across anybody as well versed at objectifying body parts as I was. In my defense, this was an occupational hazard; one of the tricks of my trade was the ability to work with whatever was at hand. Over the years I'd learned to pinpoint my focus to the width of a pubic hair if there was nothing else to work with. His voice was packed with solitude, doubt, longing. Before my eyes—or, more precisely, in my mind—Rasher became Lovely Bum Man.

I put my hands on his shoulders, to give him an actual massage. He emitted the most angelic sound, part puppy, part snowflake, part morphine. Any idea of a massage dispersed.

"Do you mind?" I asked.

The noise he made sounded a little nervous, but I felt he wasn't averse to whatever I might do.

I glanced at the door to make sure the tissue was in place, then climbed on the massage table. This tactic was used by all of the boys because of its success rate. The punter would be able to feel our thighs at either side of his hips and, conveniently, it placed our crotches directly above their bums. If the boy had any sense or experience he'd gently settle onto the cheeks below, not enough to squash the punter's bum but enough for him to realize the boy had an objective, was on target, and simply awaited further instructions.

Lovely Bum squirmed below me. He turned his head and caught my eye. For that moment the look he gave me made me love him. The permission I so badly wanted was given. I flicked the button of my shorts undone. He took over, pushing them down as far as he could reach behind his back. My dick sprang free, so hard it knocked between his bum cheeks. He sighed. Leaning on one hand as though doing a push-up, I maneuvered my shorts past my thighs to my calves, my ankles, my feet. They fell off the table, onto the floor. Completely naked, I pressed against him, knowing he was mine and would accept whatever came next.

"I don't usually fuck in here," I said. "I'll have to find a condom."

"Don't go," he said, his voice urgent but also calm.

His response confused me. "Do you not get fucked?"

"I do," he said. "Well, I used to." He paused. "What I'm saying is . . . don't use a condom."

"Sweet man," I said. "I don't know my HIV status. I haven't been tested in years."

"I want you inside me without a condom," he said calmly.

People didn't tend to admit this out loud anymore, although I felt this way myself every time I had sex and it was often implied by a course of actions. My gut shouted down any resistance, urging me to do it, but some part of me I didn't know existed told me to act responsibly.

"I pre-cum a lot when I'm excited," I warned him.

"I *want* your cum in me." I heard apology in his voice. "Please."

I couldn't believe my ears. With such good manners, how could I refuse him? I wanted to have my cum in him also. All thoughts of HIV abandoned, I put the head of my dick between the warm, smooth flesh of his cheeks.

I knelt above him, looking down at the crack of his bum cheeks. By simply remaining there he played his part perfectly. I moved my hips forward, my groin leading the way. Now the head of my dick rested on his bum hole. His body moved in a way I really liked and he made the loveliest noises. I pushed the head of my dick just past his rim, and in it went. The feeling was intense.

He clenched his fists. I loved seeing this. "Thank you, Aiden," he said sweetly.

This was the first time anybody had ever thanked me in this context. If I'd been told this as an anecdote I would have thought it odd. Now it was the most perfect thing he could have said, and the fact that he used my name made it all the more personal and beautifully tender. How fucking lucky was I?

In the last few years, whenever I'd fucked without a condom I'd always been drunk or high. I knew this was just the excuse for doing it, not the reason. Lovely Bum didn't force himself onto my shaft in a way I found too assertive. Instead he made me feel that I was being affectionate to him, not the horny fucker I'd actually become upon placing my hands on his shoulders or seeing his bum. (Who knows what the real trigger was?) My chin was now touching the back of his neck. My dick eased in farther. My blood pumped through my body as though I'd just taken a hit of poppers. I was almost all the way in him now.

I lost sense of time. The smell of candy came to mind, taking me back to when I was four years old and spending my sixpence pocket money after church on Sunday. Then back in the present, here on the massage table, my naiveté and innocence intact. The base of my dick hit home. This wasn't deep enough. If I tried harder, his cheeks would part slightly and let me go deeper. My lips touched his skin, smooth like the fabric my mother called satin. He groaned. The warmth of my cheek flat against his shoulder blades made me think of fresh-baked bread. I'd never had such arbitrary, nonsexual thoughts when lying on top of a man. Confused by internal images, my thoughts scattered in space and time, even so my dick was harder than ever. My one urge was to push it into his lovely bum that extra bit, slowly slide it out and put it in again, over and over for as long as he'd let me.

I came up his bum. He came, too.

"Please don't stop, Aiden."

How sweet he sounded. And I didn't want to stop, not after hearing him say my name again. Maybe in a moment, after a few more thrusts.

I continued to fuck. But the sensation in my balls didn't subside. At first I didn't understand what was happening, but it felt great. I wasn't about to question it. I kept going. The sensation of pressure behind my balls was building again, a promise of never-ending orgasm. This had happened before but inevitably it faded.

This time it grew and grew, far beyond where it would normally tip into orgasm. Every second that passed I thought would be the last. Still it held back.

Finally I felt a bolt of spasm, deeper in my groin than I'd ever experienced before. Surely it was impossible to make more sperm so quickly. I felt sensation traveling up my shaft.

"I'm cumming again!" I shouted.

"Oh my god! Please!" Lovely Bum was as surprised as I was.

Cum forced its way through the slit and shot out the head of my dick. It was beautifully painful. Done, spent, feeling blissful, I slumped onto Lovely Bum's back.

"Fucking hell!" I exclaimed.

My dick was still in his bum. I kissed the back of his neck. From pure joy I started to laugh. He joined me.

We continued to laugh until the force of his laughing put pressure on his gut and pushed my dick out of him.

— **4** —

After Lovely Bum I was booked for another six massages. Luckily only four of them wanted extras.

Extras meant that the customer reached orgasm. The best scenario was the standard hand job. Sometimes a punter just wanted to watch me jerk off, or pose for them in Speedos, or pretend I was part of some fantasy manly man. The list was endless of things that were effortless for me and potent for them. Some liked me to pinch their nipples while they jerked off. Others adored it if I stood over them with a hateful attitude while they looked on longingly, worshipping the crack of my bum and fearing the oppressor towering above them. One or two were happiest when I condescended to crouch down and let them sniff, smell, or—if they were lucky—savor my nutty bum hole. Customers could book half an hour, which cost them twenty-five pounds and was paid to the receptionist when the booking was made. An hour cost them forty. The boys set their own rates for extras, which were paid during the session. Management paid the boys a flat rate of twenty pounds per shift, whether or not we did any massages.

All of these four punters were hand jobs. Still, each of them sucked my dick and although it didn't get its hardest, they all seemed excited enough. This meant I only got my basic extras price of twenty-five pounds for each, a total of one hundred pounds. It was a poor day but I tried to put it in perspective. Cubus and I paid roughly one hundred fifty pounds rent per month, which we shared, so today I'd made enough to cover my rent for about a month and a half. Not so bad, really.

I finished my shift at the Burlington at six-thirty then stopped by the Ritz Hotel and was disappointed to find that Gerrick wasn't there. The money didn't concern me that much. I'd been looking forward to somebody appreciating me, flattering my intellect, understanding my sense of humor, finding me intriguing—and not diving headlong at my dick.

Gerrick had left an envelope for me with a message written on it: "I'm sorry. Something came up. Leave the script. I'll call you later." The envelope felt like it had money in it. I waited until I was out of the hotel to look inside it, and found five hundred pounds in brand-new fifty-pound notes.

Getting paid for doing nothing felt somewhat immoral. In justification, I had kept my whole evening open for Gerrick. With nothing planned I was at loose ends. I could go to a pub. The gay one in Soho was quite near. But there were only two in the West End so I was bound to see somebody I knew there. It was still Wednesday, not my best day to be around people socially. To make anybody suffer a less-than version of myself wouldn't be fair. On a practical level, the Green Park station was right beside the Ritz. *Go home*, I thought.

Seeing the stagnant faces coming out of the underground as I entered the stairwell, I had second thoughts. I went back up the few steps to the street. Kennington wasn't that far from the West End, but by tube it meant changing at Leicester Square and then drudging from the Piccadilly line to the Northern line. It was too nice an evening. I decided to walk home.

My route took me through Green Park. I picked up a copy of *Time Out* magazine at a newsstand, and when I was far enough in for the traffic to have quieted down, I sat on a park bench. Rather than search for a film that interested me and find out where it was playing, I looked up the Scala Cinema. The venue was more interesting than most and it had a gay vibe. On Saturdays they sometimes held fun all-nighters, and since all you had to do was sit there and be entertained they were much easier than a night-club. In a club I'd be constantly aware of how I held my body, where my eyes fell, what I said, what faces I made. The Scala was in Kings Cross and attracted an art house crowd in which I felt comfortable. A bonus was that you could go by yourself without feeling conspicuously alone. Between films there were breaks during which they served alcohol instead of ice cream and popcorn, and you could check out who was there. If you spoke to somebody it was because you had something to talk about. In all likelihood you both had at least one similar interest—films. More than a few times I'd ended up sitting with the person I met during intermission.

This Friday the Scala was scheduled to show *Pink Narcissus*. I'd wanted to see it for years. From everything I'd read it was a silent art house/homoerotic film, and therefore perfect for my first date with David. It might turn him on, and he would associate those feelings with me. If he found me dull, it would give him something interesting to do while he was with me. If either of us felt awkward or insecure, we wouldn't have to talk to each other too much.

The walk home took about thirty minutes. If there was anything good about the aftermath of doing drugs, it's that in addition to making me more easy to upset it made me more sensitive in a good way. I felt things more acutely, with heightened awareness. This happened now. I noticed the streams of temperature within the breeze, the hodgepodge of muddled smells, the bizarreness of nature, the River Thames and my fear of its tidal strength, the lush simplicity of a red telephone box against the blue sky. I let myself run with the images and sensations. By the time I reached Kennington I felt much better than expected for a Wednesday after doing E and coke.

The elevator in my building was out of order. I told myself to treat it as an investment. If I thought of it as a workout, I wouldn't mind the climb so much. The sixteen flights of stairs would be a great workout for my bum—money in the bank. I took two steps at a time, trying to center my body and not hold on to the banisters.

When I reached the tenth floor I came upon my neighbor from across the hallway. She had black hair and lived with her blonde sister. Both were in their late sixties. They used to be more private, but after being trapped in the elevator with me one time they'd loosened up. More than once I'd offered to carry her groceries, as I did now. Breathless, she attempted to nod; her tongue peeped out of her mouth as though looking for something besides inadequate air to fuel her. I left her shopping bags with her sister, advising her that I thought her sibling might need a cup of tea when she arrived. We damned the elevator for not working, she with clenched hands.

As I closed my front door I could see her there, listening for her sister. They only had each other. I'd have liked to be able to check in to see if they needed anything when the elevators broke down again, but I sensed that they valued their privacy and would consider it an intrusion.

My flat was quiet. No cassette or video playing. No Cubus. Was this something I had to get used to? There were no messages on my answering machine, which meant no new work possibilities but also that nobody had been trying to contact me. Alone for the evening, I felt slightly unwanted. My comedown kicked back in, pulsed into me. I found myself staring out the window at the setting sun shining on Big Ben and Parliament below me. It all looked fake. I needed a plan to fill space and time.

My evening would consist of this: watching *The Simpsons* on TV. The show had started today; I'd set my VCR to record it. After that—no, before *The Simpsons*—I'd take a warm bath and leave the bathroom window open. The breeze would feel lovely when I was wet. After that a bowl of cereal and TV. At around ten o'clock—so as not to seem too eager—I'd call David to tell him about *Pink Narcissus*.

I'd forgot to get milk. I stared at the glass on the window blankly in frustration. If I went now, before my bath, it would only take ten minutes. If I waited I wouldn't feel like doing it afterwards. Before I could change my mind I was out the door, down the stairs, over the triangle of grass that doubled as a dog toilet, and into the fluorescent lighting of the petrol station.

As I was heading back out, a funny-looking man was trying to get in the door. He looked familiar.

"Hello, Aiden," he said.

"Hey," I said, a bit spacy.

"You don't know who I am, do you."

"I recognize the face." *And the hair*, I thought.

"Heaven? Last Saturday?"

My expression must have looked blank. The petrol station lighting wasn't doing him any favors, either.

"Those E's I gave you must have been extra fine. You've well lost your memory."

What a horrible expression. "Oh, yeah, fucking hell. That was great, thanks."

"The name's Trev. I'm glad I bumped into you. I wanted to talk to you. Did you know we're neighbors? My block faces yours. I can see into your kitchen."

"You're kidding."

"Just your sink." This was said with childlike excitement.

Fucking hell! I'd washed up naked at that sink.

"You don't believe me, do you?" he said. "When you get back I'll wave."

Trev stuck with me until I reached my block. He was relentless. This wasn't about him being in an inconvenient place at an important time but about him having something horrid on me. It was as though he was the embodiment of my comedown. Trev personified a world I detested when I wasn't high. I wanted nothing to do with it.

Back inside my home, safe, I spent the evening avoiding the kitchen sink. I washed cups and plates in the bathroom. Despite Trev I was determined to have a long, relaxing bath. I brought a book with me.

Jane Austen's *Emma* fought with my own Terry for attention. Just when she'd had a "thoroughly delightful idea" about which man should meet which woman, Terry's suicide attempt pierced through and made Emma's petty vexations all the more redundant. Sadly, I could see too many parallels between her and myself, although I couldn't decide who was more self-obsessed. As my bathwater cooled to lukewarm, her mousy but persistent voice could no longer compete with the neurotic bickering monologue of my internal comedown. Why didn't I know it was Terry's birthday? If I hadn't let him leave on Sunday, if he'd stayed with me all day Monday . . . It was my fault. I shouldn't have let suicide enter his kissy, red-nosed head.

After my bath I proceeded with the evening as planned. I had a bowl of muesli and watched *The Simpsons*. The show was clever, funny, and seemed much more relevant than *Emma*. At around ten o'clock I called David. But I hadn't factored his schedule into my plan. Jezz, one of five people who shared the house, answered the phone. He told me that David had already gone to bed. To avoid playing phone tag, I asked Jezz to tell David about *Pink Narcissus* on Friday, and gave him the show time, the name of the theater, and the address. If I wasn't in when David called back he could just say yes or no. It was short notice, so he could easily get out of it with the flimsiest of excuses and I wouldn't be too hurt.

Besides meeting Trev, David being in bed—and without me—was the only crappy part of my day. Gerrick didn't call. From what little I knew of him, this seemed out of character. My thoughts and feelings were mixed and boisterous. I willed myself to sleep.

Two hours later, unsuccessful, I took some temazepam. These came as green gelcaps that most people I knew referred to as eggs. There had been talk that the British Medical Association was going to take them out of circulation because some people sucked the fluid out of the eggs with needles and injected it. How quickly did they need to get to sleep? I couldn't imagine ever wanting to inject myself with anything. My last conscious thoughts were of the Dr. Seuss book *Green Eggs and Ham*.

Thursday

— 1 —

I WAS SITTING ON THE LIVING ROOM FLOOR, MAKING a note to buy fabric to cover the kitchen window as soon as possible, when the phone beside me rang. It was Sandy from the Burlington. Cubus had called in sick and Sandy asked if I would cover for him. Officially it was my day off, but since I had missed yesterday I felt I should go in. It was an early shift, ten until three, which meant the lunchtime crowd, mostly professional types who had a good sense of time management. These were my favorite customers. We both knew our tasks and achieved them efficiently. No fuss, no mess, no game playing—they'd get off and return to their high-paid office jobs.

Maybe I had some kind of twisted work ethic myself. Whatever I was called upon to do at the Burlington, I did to the best of my ability, whether it was attending to punters or menial chores like cleaning, serving sandwiches and tea, or acting nice for the sake of the establishment. I did what I was told to by the management, which was handed down via their minions, the receptionists, who themselves referred to their own job title as management. And I did it well, maintaining my rentboy character, adding sexual flair in the massage room but trying always to be aware of how much of my actual self I gave. Surely this made me a good employee.

Still, I wondered about Cubus's "sickness." Was he taking the day off because he was sick of doing punters, or of the Burlington itself and what reflected back at him from those soul-revealing mirrors? There was no way for me to find out, because I didn't know his phone number—possibly because that was how Cubus wanted it.

I could understand Cubus's needing time off. Some days, if the boys were unlucky, every customer that chose you booked a whole hour and wanted only the massage with no extras. The Burlington still got their money for booking the massage, and so they didn't care, but all the boy would leave with was the basic wage we got paid for the whole shift and nothing for the massage. Why didn't these customers go to a proper masseur? Personally I couldn't help but resent them. If energy can pass between people, then surely I'd passed on hideous stuff during those long, strenuous, fruitless massages. Even when they did want extras, usually I didn't feel like it. There were only so many times I could act a sexy pose, jerk my dick, stick my fingers up somebody's bum, or whatever it was they needed to make them cum. Usually I felt awkward, uncomfortable, if not completely ridiculous. Try as I might to ignore my true feelings long enough to get the job done, afterwards when walking up the corridor to the kitchen to dump the cum-smeared towels I'd feel things. The equation was relatively simple. If my heart ached and my spirit was partially diminished, still it was likely to have been rewarding financially, and the more I hurt, the less inclined I was even to look in Little Fella's direction, just in case he caught my eye and made me feel ashamed, not by judging me but by quietly setting an example.

Of course if you weren't chosen at all you received no extra money, and if it happened for a few days in a row you got the sack. Therefore it was our job to make customers want extras, which entailed us doing things we generally didn't want to do. It didn't take long to learn which punters were good for extras and which ones weren't. Soon the boys knew the value of each one to the penny. It was best to be politely offhand with the customers who only wanted massages, so as not to have anybody complain about you.

Timmy, the young man on reception that morning, was well behaved and petite. The space he took up was minimal, both physically and mentally. I believe the management felt safe in thinking that he didn't have the balls to steal from the till and lacked the will to be bitchy. I couldn't comprehend how somebody could have so little spirit. I suspected he must be hiding dark secrets about himself: he clipped articles about serial killers from newspapers, or collected hair from combs left lying around the club to sniff at home later, or stayed at the Burlington all night, naked the whole time, watching porn in the TV room, eating from the fridge, and sleeping on the massage tables, using towels that hadn't been washed.

The competition was tough today. There was something for everyone, physically speaking. S was a more boyish version of myself. Kydd was much prettier than me. Wesley, a relatively new boy, was a tiny, tough blond skinhead. He wasn't the usual caliber of a Burlington boy. In reality, none of us were. We were all just pretending and although we'd never admit it to the management, most of us had "worked" places like railway stations and public toilets in department stores. Wesley had worked the streets. Worse still, he'd worked at the Earls Court Clinique, the Burlington's competition. There was something of a hardened criminal about Wesley. When he smiled or acted nice he could pass as a "lovely little thing," but he was cunty cool and infamous on the club scene as somebody not to mess with. We got on well and sometimes hung out together outside the Burlington, but I kept a safe distance.

To complete the selection of boys on show today was Mark Lawrence, always referred to by both names to distinguish him from all the other *Marks*. Mark Lawrence was beyond beautiful— tall, slim-waisted, with broad shoulders and perfectly proportioned muscles. In addition to working at the Burlington, he worked as a DJ at the Daisy Chain, a gay club night in Brixton. His father was from Cuba and his mother from Yorkshire, and they had produced a specimen the many cricket and private-school types that frequented the Burlington would call "a colored chap." Apparently Mark's race scared them, however physically perfect he might be. Admittedly I wasn't that popular with the private-school types either. They demanded that you have no personality, be servile, and grateful to them for honoring you with their business. They would choose me every now and then because of the size of my dick, but they knew they'd have to suffer the personality that unfortunately came with it.

I hoped that some of my regulars would show up. On good days customers booked me solid for half-hour massages all the way through my shift and always wanted extras. Somebody from the highly illusive and always invisible management had been in and as a result the receptionists were at their most military, wiping fingers on surfaces to check for dust, peering into mirrors for smudges, and sticking their heads in toilet cubicles to make sure there were no skid marks. I had a certain amount of immunity from their scrutiny because generally I raked in money for the club.

As it turned out, today was a good day for all the boys. Everyone working was busy. The only chance any of us had to talk was in passing, as we threw towels in the bins or headed towards the front desk to find out about our next booking. I breezed through the shift without having to perform a single housekeeping chore.

I showered, dressed, and was ready to leave the Burlington at about ten minutes after three. As I picked up the book I'd left in the kitchen, I bumped into Mark Lawrence. He looked so cool and sexy, with little red football shorts on and no socks. This made his legs seem really long, but because they were so muscular and defined he looked stunning.

"Mark!"

"Aiden," he said, pulling off a yellow singlet.

"You look gorgeous!"

He made a cute *aw-shucks* expression.

"I was just modeling for Jean-Paul Gaultier," he explained, "and wanted to look good, so I did a few steroid shots. Not much. Just enough to sculpt me a bit."

"*Jean-Paul Gautier*. Get you."

"I've done quite a few shows in Paris. Little good it does me. I can still earn more down here in a day."

"It's been good today."

"Yeah, great."

S marched into the kitchen disgruntled, very unlike himself. He threw towels into the bin and sighed dramatically. "Don't ask!" he said to our inquiring glances, and stomped back out.

"That's how I felt earlier," Mark said.

"I don't envy you," I responded. "But look at the bright side. If it stays this busy, you'll make enough cash to *buy* Thailand."

"Make that one Thai to go," he said in an American accent, grinning.

I laughed, more out of feeling nice than finding the joke funny. It was difficult not to feel good around Mark. He exuded the same lovability as puppies and kittens. You couldn't help adoring him.

"When are you leaving?" I asked.

"In two days. I can't wait."

"Then what are you doing here?"

"I'm not done yet. I'm on till six."

There was some commotion at the front desk, a customer complaining about the cost of membership. Mark and I disregarded it.

"Don't you have packing to do?" I continued.

"All packed already, but you can never have enough cash when traveling."

Finally I shifted the conversation to what I really wanted to talk about.

"I hear Cubus is looking after your place."

"Yeah. He's doing me a real favor. If anybody noticed it was empty, the place would be cleared out in days."

"I haven't heard from Cubus for a while."

"I don't see that much of him either. He keeps to himself."

I gave up.

"Do me a favor, Mark, and put your shirt on. I can't think straight looking at you like that."

Embarrassed again, he slipped on a vibrant blue T-shirt.

"Great color against your skin, but what's with the different outfit?"

"Costume change never hurts. It's funny, but a punter will suddenly notice me who's been looking through me all day."

"How could anybody miss you? You're the only black guy who sets foot in the club, let alone works here."

"I don't begin to try and figure out the mind of a punter, but a change always works. I've got a white tracksuit for later, and a cap."

"I'm off now. I'll see you in a few months."

"You heading home?"

"Not yet. I've got a private job in Eardley Crescent."

"Father Michael?"

"The very same."

"He's a riot. Have fun."

"I'm expecting to."

My shift at work had gone well financially but it had been dull, so I was glad to be seeing Father Michael. He'd called right after I told Sandy I would cover Cubus's shift, and asked me to pop into the vicarage for "tea" at four o'clock. The timing worked perfectly. But first I planned to go around the corner to the Ritz. Father Michael and I knew each other well enough that he wouldn't mind if I was a little late, but I didn't have much time.

I ran the short distance to the hotel's grand front entrance. I managed to get the attention of the same woman who had given me Gerrick's previous message. She moved in my direction, touching the elbow of her colleague to let her know she was dealing with me. This made me smile. She smiled back.

Raising her eyebrows, she said, "Mr. Boden, wasn't it?"

Past tense. Was that a highbrow way of speaking I didn't know about?

"Your memory is excellent," I said.

With the skill of a great actor she managed to express both satisfaction and humility. Then she looked at me sincerely and said, "Mr. Boden left this morning."

Surprised, I said, "Did he leave any messages?"

She shook her head.

It seemed odd that Gerrick would leave without telling me. But that wasn't my first thought. Initially what went through my mind was, *What a dear woman, it looks like she cares, how lovely.*

– **2** –

The Mass. A Bible with onionskin pages. The smell of frankincense. A long black robe and white collar. A priest. Any one of these things had the ability to snatch me back to being five years old. During Stations of the Cross, choir practice, or confession, there you'd find

Little Fella, a good boy, holy and proud, but not so full of Pride that God would frown. Treasured memories. Dear Little Fella.

Some things never change. Now I knelt before a priest again, in prayer once more, but my prayer was that the other rentboy would arrive soon. My stored pool of sexy religious allusions was nearly exhausted. With Father Michael Hekram it was all about the visuals, so I couldn't resort to getting him to suck me off. This was surprising considering that he worshipped dicks, the bigger the better. But he never touched me. We didn't even shake hands. Perhaps he thought he was keeping a chaste distance.

For two and a half years I'd been going to the house in Eardley Crescent every couple of months. I'd gotten to know Father Michael slightly, but not the most obvious things. I knew little about his physicality, as he never got undressed. His tummy must have been large, from the shape it made in his cassock. I knew he kept a parrot in the kitchen where you entered from the steps leading from the street into the basement. His sermons and way of preaching were a mystery to me. My curiosity did almost push me to sit in the back of St. Finbar's Anglican Church to hear one, but I decided against it. Better not to fuck with Little Fella's head too much.

I did know about Father Michael's sexual fantasies and his love of the almighty dick. When he called me I knew I was in for a good time. My imagination was profoundly embroiled in repression, but obviously not as much as a priest's. Once Father Michael got going I could almost smell his intensity, and the fact that he never took off his collar or cassock added a naughty devilishness.

Around fifteen minutes after I arrived my prayer was answered by a six-foot-something, chalk-white blond. He moved towards me like a massive ocean wave—slow, loaded with power, a little threatening—with one huge hand extended.

"Dagur," he said, his jaw dropping caveman-like as he pronounced the *gur*.

Suddenly I felt too evolved. Surely this primitive beast wouldn't have a clue what to do with a high-tech calculator. Luckily I was able to multitask enough to put together a word.

"Aiden," I replied.

Not that he'd asked. Without further ado he flicked open the buttons of his tight, brand-new dark-blue jeans and peeled them apart, revealing a weighty bulge in his washed-out green briefs. With a few jagged movements he shed these and began to undo my jeans. I pulled off my T-shirt. Now superhero and I were good to go. In fact, I was *raring* to go.

We did exactly what Father Michael told us to. Admittedly these were hardly joyless chores. All the time he kept his cassock hitched up with one hand and pinched at his nodule dick with the fingertips of the other, frantically jerking himself between his thick white legs.

Dagur and I put our faces together.

"Don't kiss," said Father Michael.

We slid our faces against each other, our lips moving across each other's forehead, hair, ears, neck. I breathed in through my nose to capture the scent of Dagur's skin. When I breathed out I placed the breath close to his skin, hoping it would achieve the same effect on him that his hot breath had on me. The fact that I couldn't kiss him made it much more fervent, adding a held-back, desperate longing. Every now and then Father Michael bent in like a cherry-picker camera seeking to catch all angles. But he never touched us.

"Rub Aiden," he instructed.

As his excitement mounted, he spewed commands, interspersed with excited exclamations.

"Aiden, suck him . . . Awh! Dagur, run your hand over Aiden's back. Worr! Now his buttocks . . . Oh! Oh! Oh! Aiden, hold both your dicks together and wank them."

Bless him.

"Dagur, suck Aiden's balls."

This was too good to be true. It was like having a guardian angel making sure that everything I wanted actually happened.

"I can't hold back much longer," I said.

"Oh yes. Yes, yes. You cum, cum yes."

I looked down at Dagur to see how he felt about this. He nodded slowly, imperceptible to Father Michael. This was all I needed. Just looking into his eyes had started my balls churning.

My body tensed. Cleverly Dagur pushed his face into my balls, thereby ensuring my orgasm was intense and avoiding my cum, which burst from the tip of my dick and soared past his head and over his shoulder.

The sight of me cumming sent Father Michael into another, more heightened level of exhilaration.

"Awh . . . magnificent! Absolutely splendid. Now you, Dagur. Aiden, kneel down, kneel down." As if I needed telling twice. "Now suck him!"

I was happy to comply. Before I put his dick in my mouth I looked up at Dagur, wanting to capture the moment, to lock it inside me for further jerk-off material. With a blink I imprinted the memory—his powerful legs, his heavy jaw empty of expression, Dagur's weighty dick—as though taking a photograph of it. He must have wondered what I was waiting for, because he took hold of the back of my head.

"Put it in, Dagur!" squealed Father Michael.

He hovered like a flying beetle, his black cassock flapping as he darted here then there. His excitement increased my own.

"Cum on, Aiden!"

Pretending that I could put on a better show, I held my face steady in front of Dagur's dick. I wanted his cum on me.

Dagur's eyes widened. His mouth opened, froze. I braced myself. He turned his head to one side, so that his chin was over his shoulder.

"Whoa! Here we go," he announced, his voice even lower than usual.

Globs of juicy cum pumped out of his dick. I wanted to leave my mouth open, to swallow it all. Instead, acting the professional, I closed it, as if I were a careful, clean whore. But something inside me wouldn't let me miss this. I pretended I didn't know more was coming, that I was saying *fucking hell*—and it shot into my mouth. For the first time ever, cum actually had a milky taste. It was lovely, warm as though it sat on hot porridge, both sweet and salty.

I told myself to grimace, look disgusted.

Dagur didn't see this; he still had his head to one side. He kept cumming. It pumped out, landing on my chin, my neck, my nose, my forehead. I held his cum in my mouth, not wanting to waste it by swallowing. Not yet. He mustn't have cum for a week. If I wasn't so experienced I might have thought the quantity bizarre, but luckily I had the luxury of being a prostitute. I wallowed in his cum, my mouth closed now, breathing through my nose, once again pretending that I was avoiding his cum whereas in reality I wanted to smell it.

He jerked slower and slower, milking the last of his climax from his groin.

Now it was Father Michael's turn. With a high-pitched, tweeting sound he came into a tissue.

Within seconds he resumed his priestly persona, getting us out of the vicarage as quickly, politely, and with as little fuss as possible, so that he could return to his pastoral duties at St. Finbar's Anglican Church.

Dagur and I walked to the underground together. Ordinarily I would have taken a cab home, but I had not yet had my fill of this Nordic deity. It was still rush hour and we had to stand. I managed to position myself so that I stood in the curl between Dagur's hand and head as we held on to the handrail. If the tube stopped suddenly

I would have fallen into him and his arm would be around me. I wanted nothing more than to lean into him and kiss his face. If I could help it this wouldn't be the last I saw of him.

But I had to take it slowly. We didn't know each other.

In an attempt to remedy this I quizzed him as subtly as I able to, asking him simple questions like where he'd come from and where he lived now. He answered, but his tone didn't suggest he was interested in having a conversation. Maybe he just wasn't chatty, I reasoned, or it was some kind of Nordic reserve, a cultural thing. Perhaps my questions were just too dull for him.

I asked what he did for fun, what clubs he liked.

He didn't like clubs.

He must have a boyfriend. Probably they preferred to stay at home with each other.

No, this also was wrong.

Finally he told me he'd just gotten engaged to a hot German woman.

Now everything made horrible sense.

I arrived home to find a message from David on my answering machine.

"Yes," he said, and paused, I assume being funny. Then, "I'll meet you outside the cinema at eight."

Yes! I thought. *Fuck straight men.*

One of the good things about living on the sixteenth floor—aside from the view and the fact that heavy metals from car exhaust can only rise three feet—was that it was too high up to hear any noise from the street (unless somebody screamed, which sometimes happened). Kennington wasn't the best of areas but I couldn't imagine anybody being able to scale the featureless sides of my concrete building to get to my bedroom. This meant that, weather permitting, I could sleep with the windows open and feel safe. Which is exactly what I did.

Friday

— 1 —

I WOKE TO A WEIRD SMELL COMING FROM OUTSIDE. I leaned over in bed and peered out the window, but couldn't detect what the smell was.

I thought of Gerrick. What had happened? Thank god I'd photocopied the script. I'd never be able to reconstruct it from memory. In all probability Gerrick would get in touch next time he came to London. Still, how could I have been so naïve? Why does anybody call a rentboy? What was I thinking? That he liked me? Be realistic, Aiden, I told myself. You know your value to the penny and it's measured in inches, time, age, stamina, looks, and being able to put up with gross and sometimes bizarre situations. Personality was far down on a much longer list, and even farther down came intelligence. You should have insisted on having sex.

What if Gerrick was embarrassed because my writing was so bad? I didn't need to hear that unless he could give me helpful advice. It might be better if he didn't contact me again. Best to simply file him in memory as somebody who came and went, like most of the other punters I'd met in nearly three years as a rentboy.

Maybe I just felt jaded today and should blame it on that smell.

Nobody rang from the Burlington to ask me to come in. All I had to do today was prepare, plan, worry, and get nervous about meeting David. This date was a long time coming and I wanted to look my best. What I needed was a haircut and a good workout at the YMCA. But I was in no rush to get out of bed.

Cool morning air, smelling slightly weird, blew in my window. I picked up *Emma*, and after another two chapters I thought Jane Austen must be clever to make me think her character so tedious. I persisted for a couple of hours, until the telephone rang. Then I had to get up, to answer it.

"Hey," I said, using my working voice. If it wasn't a punter my friends would know it was an act; a date would probably think it sexy and my mum would assume I had a cold.

"Hey, yourself."

The voice sounded friendly and a bit cheeky.

"Who's that? Do I know you?"

"It's Lionel, and no you don't. But I think we should meet," he said.

I followed suit. "You do, do you?"

"Yeah," he said, cocky now. "How's about you come over to my pad?"

"Where would that be?"

"In Acton."

Not an area of London I was familiar with. "When were you thinking?"

"This afternoon?"

I scribbled down the directions. Ordinarily I would have asked him lots of questions. Unknown to punters, I tended to interview them. My gut feeling was that it wasn't necessary with this man. His voice had Cockney Santa Claus warmth to it, which I liked.

The corresponding visual of Saint Nicholas naked wasn't particularly sexy but it was harmless. It shouldn't be that difficult to spend a little time with him. And if it resulted in me shooting a load of cum this afternoon, then I wouldn't be too horny when I saw David. I already knew I wanted more than just one date with him, and from my experience there was no surer way of making this happen than letting him feel my dick, preferably hard from his having caused it, then not sleep with him. It might confuse him, and I hoped it would frustrate him, but I'd bet money he'd want to see me again.

I got off the tube at Acton Town and followed Lionel's directions: take a right out of station past cinema, left at chip shop, orange door, number three, press buzzer. That was easy enough, I reassured myself, acknowledging that the journey had been painless. The intercom system looked grubby. Not wanting to get my fingers dirty I used my elbow to press it. The piercing electronic screech that resulted sounded like a recording of a pterodactyl.

Hissing, a crackling pause, then a robot clearing its throat.

"Aiden?"

I recognized the voice. Lionel sounded genuinely excited. I already felt appreciated.

"Lionel?" I said.

"Come on up."

Opening the door I encountered a flight of stairs covered with off-white wool carpet, expensive but a bit 1970s. Lionel greeted me on the first landing.

"Hello, fella!"

My imagination hadn't been far wrong. There *was* something Santa Claus about him. He wore a fleece tracksuit that consisted of baggy trousers with an elastic waistband and a zip-up jacket.

"Come in, come in. Welcome to my home."

He even spoke in Christmas song lyrics. The main difference

was that the red had been tuned down. His face, which shone a lovely smile, lacked the rosy hue that ordinarily would accompany such cheeks.

"Can I get you anything?" he asked.

"What have you got?" I said.

"Well, I shouldn't have much of it, because I'm diabetic, but I have some whiskey."

A drink shouldn't affect me that much, I reasoned—my stomach was pretty full—and it might even help. It would ease my anxiety about David and it might make me tolerable for Lionel.

"Whiskey sounds good."

He clapped his hands together gleefully.

"That's my fella!"

Funny that he chose this name. He used it in the same way some use *dear*, *sweetie*, or *love*, implying not so much intimacy as familiarity with somebody you don't know.

"Sit! Sit! Sit! Please!" he said.

To my left was a grand old leather chair. An image of me sitting in it looking like a whiz kid CEO of some multinational company came to mind. This couldn't have been further from what I was or would ever be. Liking the picture of myself in this alternate reality, I sat down in the chair.

Lionel shuffled over to a cabinet at the far end of his large sitting room. "How do you take it?" he asked.

"I don't *take it*," I said confidently.

"You've a sense of humor, haven't you?" he said, picking up on my irony and obvious double meaning. "But seriously, how would you like it?"

"Straight up!"

Ice chinked in his glass. He gave me a meaningful look.

"Honestly, I like my whiskey straight up."

"I like you, Aiden," he said, and set about preparing my drink.

When meeting a punter for the first time I was always slightly wary. Instinctively my gut took over and made decisions for me. Some would call this street smarts, others intuition. My mother would say it was just being sensible. Regardless of what you called it, it kicked in immediately. I scanned the room quickly, trying to learn about Lionel from his home. My life might depend on it.

Clues. A piano. Although everyone I knew had one when I was growing up, it wasn't common these days. Framed photos of famous-looking people. Having studied photography at college I noticed that they didn't look like publicity shots. They were more personal, as though the subjects had a relationship with the photographer. Lionel must be in show business. Although clearly expensive, most things in the room appeared worn, as though times had once been better.

Lionel took me out of these thoughts by handing me a drink.

"There you go, Aiden."

"Cheers," I said.

It may have been just a word, but years of study on what macho is and how it's done convincingly had gone into my one-word piece of amateur dramatics.

Fooled, Lionel smiled at me. "You're a good kid," he said, tousling my hair. "I can tell."

I took exception to being called a kid—after all, I *was* twenty-three—but it's difficult to dislike somebody who thinks well of you. I found myself enjoying his company.

He gestured around the room with his eyes. "I should look after the place better."

"It's nothing a housekeeper couldn't sort out in . . ." I paused for comedic effect, with the level of cheek I thought acceptable based on our first few words on the phone. "Let's just say a few hours." For some reason I added a lie. "Mine's the same."

In reality my flat tended to be military-precision neat.

Tidying up was my method of dealing with comedowns, a way of bringing order out of chaos or at least behaving like a good boy.

Lionel gazed into his drink. "I should look after *myself* better," he said. He seemed to be speaking to himself.

His candor impressed me, and touched me. In that moment I believed I saw the man before me with more real eyes than my own, or from a more emotionally evolved place. Maybe it was part of the comedown, the aftermath of whatever was in the E's I'd taken. Maybe it was just my imagination. Whichever it was, I knew I felt different. Lionel was no longer just some punter in a weary flat in Acton Town. He was somebody who needed me, for whatever and for however long. I accepted him. He had a greatness about him, like he was *somebody* in the world, or deserved to be. Some writer should document him for posterity. He wasn't going to last much longer. For all his warmth, openness, and generosity of spirit, he was beat up and too full of sorrow.

"Aiden, here's the deal," he said, as though I'd asked him a question. "To be frank, my dick doesn't really rise to the occasion anymore, if you know what I mean."

With aged deliberation, he shook his head. My eyes seemed to register this in slow motion, and on the way to my brain I turned his shaking head into something symbolic: a profound disappointment, more than at simply not being able to get it up, something to do with loss of health and youth and lots of other stuff about his life.

He looked me in the eye. "But, Aiden, I still get great pleasure in it all."

My mouth was open, sipping my drink. I lowered the glass self-consciously, simultaneously closing my mouth, and in doing so felt more dignified.

Despite my silly concerns with my actions, he said, "You know. The looking. The touching. The whole goddamn experience." He lowered his head, took a large theatrical gulp of his neat whiskey. "I miss that part of my life."

Then, behaving like the cliché of a tired, washed-up Hollywood has-been, he clenched his fist and made the minutely measured motion of slowly pounding his knee in a way that made me want to be able to comfort him, soothe him, and simply help him somehow.

Finally he looked up at me. His eyes flickered to my crotch. My dick pulsed.

He looked away as though nothing had happened, continuing to talk, but it was more like he was thinking out loud. Way ahead of him, I undid my zipper slowly, waiting for him to notice. When he didn't look I paused, holding the zipper with my forefinger and thumb.

His eyes swung up at me again. I made a jerking movement with my head to get his attention. He did a double take. With his eyes on mine I redirected them to my crotch and unzipped my fly all the way.

He returned his head to where it had been, facing his drink, but kept his eyes covertly on my fly, his gaze sly, as though my crotch was forbidden fruit. I found this sexy. I knew I had his full attention. Now I had to shake him loose, do whatever it took to set him free from the memory of his former life.

Drawing on my experience as a rentboy, I conjured up from inside myself the stripper, the dancing bear, the inside-out bearded freak boy. But this should in no way be associated with me being tacky. My intention was not to put on a show, swinging clothing around my head and grinding my hips, but to celebrate my body for Lionel, to bare myself like a new lover revealing areas of his skin that people wouldn't normally see, and then more private areas of the body, parts that nobody would see unless sex was involved. Showing these body parts was special, it *meant* something—something utterly precious.

With careful consideration I undressed. When I was completely naked, he summoned me over to him with a simple hand gesture.

I'm often surprised by what works for me sexually. It's as though there's a completely different set of rules for normal life and sex that don't correspond at all. Often they don't have a clue what each other is trying to communicate, wants, or needs. Merely being there naked with Lionel turned me on.

It became clear that all that was required of me was that I stand beside him while he looked at me. I know about these things, and I can say without doubt that he wasn't lascivious or lecherous. Lionel, an ancient soul with a trashed heart, didn't kneel or grovel or become a subservient pig. It wouldn't suit him. Lionel was too majestic for that. Deep inside him there was a dignity that self-pity couldn't touch. He was great despite himself. With me naked beside him he became what I believe was his true self—easy, breezy, carefree. More importantly he was loving, caring, and—my absolute favorite—enthusiastic in a calm, laid-back way.

He stroked my legs, which made me feel very sexy. Quietly and without fuss he loved me being there and naked with him. A couple of times he took hold of the base of my dick but didn't jerk it. He simply held his hand still with a firm, manly grip, as though my existing near him was enough. I was lovely to him just as I was, no tricks, no forcing this or that. Having his arm around my waist was all he wanted or needed for now. This tapped into how I often felt with lovers. There didn't always have to be sucking or fucking or even kissing. Just having my lips pressed against their faces was beyond amazing. I sensed that Lionel was doing this now, and I appreciated it so much I wanted to give him more. But it wasn't necessary. This was enough.

After about twenty minutes he said, "You get dressed now, if you like. You must feel a right idiot standing around naked in a room in Acton with a silly old man."

"Being naked is my occupation. I don't feel an idiot and I don't think you're silly."

"Even when I do this?" he pressed his face against my leg.

'It's lovely."

"My dear boy. It's you who are lovely." He looked at me, his eyes starting to water. "Can I see you again?"

I took his face in my hands. "You'd better!"

His face beamed.

"Don't you want to cum?" I asked.

"I'm good," he said. "Cumming won't satisfy anything. Not truly."

Put like that, I had to agree. What a huge task to undertake: to try to satisfy oneself truly. My head spun. Nothing satisfies truly. I shuddered at how bleak the world he inhabited might be.

"You'd better stick your clothes on, mate."

He patted my bum as I turned to retrieve them from the sofa. I found this adorable, because I knew he was so gentle.

"You got places to go now, people to see?" he asked.

It was unlike customers who checked their watches to see exactly how many minutes I'd spent with them and then accused me with "Going already?" Lionel's "people and places" sounded like a hip expression from the Sixties. I also sensed he wanted, in some small way, to live life through me.

"I was just planning to go to the gym, then see a film later," I said. It seemed kinder not to mention that it was a date, in case it hurt him in any way.

"Do you have time for another drink?"

"Yeah. I kind of like you."

"There's my fella! I like you too, Aiden."

Back in the CEO chair, I asked, "Are you famous, Lionel?"

"It depends if you know anything about musical theater."

"Fill me in," I said.

He spoke with his back to me while he prepared our drinks. This was tactical, because what he told me shocked me. Had I heard of him? Of course I had. Well, the musical anyway.

"Wow!" I gushed. "Really."

He nodded in a practical, unaffected way.

"My sister was in one of your shows at school. I'm not a musicals type, but *Oliver!* is probably my all-time favorite. I love it. I know nearly all the songs by heart."

"Stop," Lionel said, turning around and wafting his hand downwards. "I don't believe you."

"I've cried at that film so many times."

"I *was* pleased with the screen adaptation. Great casting."

"You must still make a lot of money from that."

He sighed. "It's funny what life deals us," he said in a surprisingly light way. "A boyfriend of mine sold it to buy drugs back in the Seventies."

"Do you still see him?" I asked hesitantly.

"No." Lionel stared straight ahead at nowhere in particular, lost in thought. He pursed his lips slightly and then smiled. It reassured me that the internal scenario had a happy ending. "Too many drugs," he said casually.

"I'm sorry," I said, and meant it.

"He was no good."

We fell silent. Then Lionel flipped the page in his mental book.

"What do you do, Aiden? Besides this. You're obviously a smart kid."

"I studied Expressive Arts at Polytechnic."

"Tell me what that means exactly."

"It covers both visual and performing arts."

"You did some acting?"

"It was more about expression. We had movement classes. It sounds so ridiculous and outdated. Anyway, I only did a year."

"Why did you stop?"

"Money. And they weren't teaching me anything. I can move around in my living room and paint and draw there too. I couldn't see why I needed to pay some establishment to do it."

"I hear you. I never had any formal training. And do you do those things in your living room now?"

"The only creative thing I do now is write."

"Really. What"

"Just bits and pieces. The only complete thing I've written is a screenplay."

"At your age that's pretty good."

"You can't say that. You haven't read it."

"So bring it next time you come—I mean, if that's okay."

"Of course it's okay. If my sister knew you were reading my screenplay, she'd faint."

Lionel chuckled. He was obviously used to such adulation but took it with good humor. We sat in silence for a moment.

I swallowed the last of my drink. "I'd better be off," I said, getting up.

"Very good, Aiden." Lionel pulled a wad of cash from his tracksuit. "Here's your dosh. You're worth every penny. And take this." He gave me an additional couple of twenties, and hesitated with a third. "I can't take this stuff seriously." He gave me two more. "Like I said, you're a good fella. There ain't any like you in this city."

"Thank you, Lionel."

"I want to make sure you come back."

"Don't worry, Lionel, I will."

– **2** –

The café in the West End YMCA overlooked the gym and multiuse court area where teenagers now played basketball. I hoped the caffeine in my black coffee would knock the whiskey out of my system.

The boys had my attention—their colorful shorts and vests, their physicality, beauty, and skill, the complexity of their communication. They were ideal entertainment, like a good film, only the plot was more complex and subtle, more profound and affecting. The boys swaggered like powerful yet graceful great cats, their fluid movements loaded with energy. I watched their springing leaps and speeding sprints, their heavy hands and feet flapping, their eyes sizing up the ball, the net, their team members, themselves and everybody who'd become spellbound by them. Were they being competitive or showing off? My favorite player caught a pass. He ducked and swerved, faked a pass, then stopped. He attempted a shot that defied the laws of physics. The ball fell short. This wasn't important. He'd attempted something magnificent and everybody felt it. There was something different in his walk now—a loser's cool, boastful pride.

Often gay men were well-groomed, had the best physiques, wore the hippest clothes, and were the only ones who laughed in serious, macho places such as a gym. But compared to these boys we were aesthetic travesties. One effortless breath, smile, yawn, or sulk from these creatures cast us into the shadows, putting some of us to shame. I was never the kind of gay who fantasized about straight men, believing them to be more masculine and therefore more desirable. When it came to being male, gays nailed it for me. But teenage boys were on a whole different level, unspoken about.

Gertrude Stein wrote, "What is the use of being a boy if you grow up to become a man, what is the use?" Too quickly I made a comparison between Lionel being satisfied to have me in his sight and what I was doing now with these boys. As I had with Lionel, I justified my behavior as harmless.

I changed into my shorts and crossed the edge of the court to get to the stretch mats. I didn't fancy pushing myself with a strenuous workout, so I decided to do a half hour on the bicycle. The alarm on my watch went off. Distracted, I stepped onto the court without looking where I was going.

Immediately somebody tumbled into me. We both fell to the ground. He landed on top of me and clumsily rolled off. I burst out laughing. This may have been the effect of the whiskey or simply that it was good to have physical contact with the boy. The scent of fresh sweat wafted off him and went straight to my balls. I noticed the lovely smell of washing powder warmed by a body.

The boy jumped to his feet and offered his hand to help me up, apologizing again and again. I blamed myself for not looking, even as I was disappointed that the tumbler wasn't my favorite boy. I'd have loved any interaction with *him*. All of the boys were looking at us. My eyes scanned the court. My favorite was watching. Something in his gaze registered in my gut.

The bicycles overlooked the court but I'd have to crane my head to keep looking at my favorite. This would not only be uncomfortable, it would be creepy. I settled into *Emma*. After thirty minutes I was only a few pages from the end so I kept peddling until I finished the book. By the time I crossed the court again the basketball game was over and the boys had gone.

Their noise and smell hit me when I entered the locker room. The boys were changing into their school uniforms. It was impossible not to notice trousers being pulled up over underpants, hands tucking in shirts front and back. Here and there some boy bent to tie a shoelace or put on a sock. My locker was in the dead center of them. I wasn't about to wait until they finished so I moved forward, determined not to be intimidated, and excused my way through them to my locker.

Then I toyed with their curiosity. Surrounded by boys, I

lifted off my T-shirt. Compared to theirs my body was muscular, so I did this with a fair amount of confidence. By the time I pulled down my shorts, my dick had enough blood in it to make it look impressive. I coughed, paused, coughed again, and reached for my towel in the back of my locker. If my adolescence was anything to go by, it's likely they were as hyperaware of me being a full-grown man as I was of their youth. Moving through them again with my towel held casually in front of my crotch but not hiding it, I headed towards the showers. Their pack mentality switched over to a more placid herding as the boys meandered out of the locker room in one long stream.

I had the showers to myself. Perfect. For me showering was about cleaning my body. I preferred to do this practical task with as little interaction with anybody else as possible. I set about washing myself—neck, back, armpits, dick, bum. I bent over to wash my feet, paying particular attention to the spaces between my toes. When I came back up I faced the showerhead, letting the water flow over me. Some days the water merely felt wet. Today it was a sensual mix of medicine and magic. Gradually I realized that somebody else had come into the room and was at the shower immediately behind my back and bum. Feeling vulnerable, I turned around.

The person behind me was just rotating away, turning slowly to face the wall. It felt like a performance. More importantly, it was my favorite boy from the court. I was dumbstruck.

Naked he was beyond perfect. I wondered if he'd turned away to hide his dick. In doing so he gave me the view I preferred, of his bum. There was nobody else in the showers to see me, so I allowed myself to enjoy the spectacle. It would be a crime not to. When would I ever get to see something so precious again?

My Boy lathered his body and washed his bum hole. (Of course I focused on this.) When he rinsed, he moved his hand back towards his bum and left his fingers resting in the crack. If only he knew the affect he had on me. He probably didn't have a clue. There was no way he could begin to conceive what he did to my brain, my groin, my heart, my very spirit. At his age surely he was unaware of anything sexual. Fortunately I never had to worry about getting hard in the showers. I'm just not wired that way. After all, it was a public place, not a sexual one. I'd as soon expect to get turned on while shopping in a crowd of people. Even so my dick impressed me by not springing up rigid and pulsing now. It seemed my excitement was more cerebral than physical. Would my dick lie? I don't think it had the ability. It had with punters, thousands of times, but that was different. With them I was pretending, thinking of things that truly turned me on. Perhaps I was just kidding myself.

Several minutes passed. I continued facing straight ahead, my eyes feasting on My Boy. Like a more classy lap dancer he slid his fingers slowly up and down the crack of his bum. His other hand disappeared in front of him at crotch level. I could only fantasize what it was doing. I suppressed the desire to drop to my knees and worship him.

How prettily the water trickled down his back. Why did the water from my showerhead pour fast and gray yet his flow in slow motion, silvery gold with glittering highlights? His soft bum hair caught the water and held it a moment before it allowed itself to drop off. No wonder the water wouldn't let go: What thing in this universe wouldn't want to stay there as long as possible?

Just when I was about to give up and leave the room, fearing I wouldn't be able to take any more without losing my mind, my dignity, or my freedom to stay out of prison, My Boy turned his face towards me till it was just over his left shoulder. I backed into my shower a little, not wanting to be caught drooling. He continued to turn, twisting his torso slightly, and stopped. His tongue brushed the tip of fluff above his top lip, and again he rubbed the crack of his bum, deeper this time, with more intent.

Was I mistaken, clueless, fucked up from two glasses of whiskey? Desperately my brain did the math. I was twenty-three. He was sixteen, fifteen, at worst fourteen. There was less than ten years difference in our ages. I'd dated men much more than ten years older than me.

My Boy brought his other hand behind him and ever so subtly pulled his cheeks apart, just a touch but enough. The water flowed over him and now I could see how sensual it was. When it fell from his bum it must taste like nutty caramel at the heavenly temperature of cum. Clever, beautiful, lucky water. The liquid nothingness had never seemed so worthy of my jealousy.

Fuck it. I tried to work things out in the conscious, overused, increasingly irritating rational part of my brain, and in doing so convince myself that there was just cause for what was likely to happen next. Lionel was forty years my senior . . . silly Art at least another ten . . . that made fifty . . .

My Boy continued facing to the side, somewhat in my direction.

What was stopping me? Morality? I don't think so. I'd never quite seen eye to eye with that tired old bitch. The law? Damn the law. Nobody was around; I'd hear them if they were. For once the annoying amplification of noises in the locker room would be a good thing, work in my favor. Surely this was a sign.

Step towards him, you fool, I told myself. *This is the chance in a lifetime. Do it.* "You are hereby sentenced to life imprisonment," said another part of my brain. My deliberations tormented me.

My Boy turned his head more, and his torso, until he was looking straight at me. Golden water flickered over his eyelashes. His perfect kissable lips and deep mouth smiled with a boyishness that made me blush, considering what was running through my head. It was all over now. Having had his outrageously cheeky fun he was probably going to leave casually, as though at this moment he wasn't the most important thing in my life.

But no. He shifted his weight once more and began turning his whole body. The tip of his dick came bobbing into view. From the height of it, he had to have a hard-on. It took all my will not to look at it. I pictured myself deep-throating him to the point of gagging. Lazy and comfortable, he completed his turn.

The cheekiness of the young. Twenty years ago he could have been arrested for being naked in public showers.

What harm could it do to look? Maybe destiny wasn't just a lazy, slightly druggy way of enabling people to put up with things. If this was *destiny* then it was out of my hands, beyond my control. (Like that would stick in a court of law.) I looked at his dick.

Jesus Christ! Before me was the dick that God had made for Adam. It didn't have veins, wasn't blue or even red but just a creamy pink color, the same as his face. It looked brand-new. It stood straight up, fully hard, firm and rigid against his tummy. He smiled at me as though it was the most natural thing in the world.

Back up, I told myself. Did his hard dick have anything to do with me? Maybe this always happened to him in the showers, or he was from some civilized country where nudity wasn't sinful or disgusting and hard-ons were nothing to be embarrassed or ashamed about. Perhaps his smile was just expressing, *Oops, it's happened again. Mum says it's my age.*

Even if I had caused it, I couldn't assume that it was an invitation. It was *his* sexuality and arousal, not *ours*. Then again, as soon as he showed me his hard-on didn't it then become ours? He didn't have to turn around. He could have just reached for his towel and dried himself without exposing himself to me.

As the scarily biblical voice in my head debated with the terrifyingly medieval feeling in my gut, My Boy stroked the golden wisps leading down to his pubic hair, placing his dick in front of his hand. There was nothing significant about this action but my whole body absorbed it. Any action he made might have had the same affect on me. My world was all about him now. His other hand rubbed his chest lightly, where the hair had sprung up in patches like freshly sewn grass seedlings. The only thing missing was a soundtrack playing, so dreamlike was he, so filmic the whole visual.

A door slammed open in the locker room. "Engel! Get your bleeding arse into gear," came the caricature voice used by all Phys.-Ed. teachers. The volume of this cry shocked me and the visual that went with it was disturbing. Bleeding arse? Ouch!

"Coming, sir," said My Boy. Again a double meaning, but this time much more pleasing.

The door slammed shut. Once again splashing water was the only sound. Teacher had gone.

My Boy didn't seem too fazed by the interruption. He pulled a resigned face, parted his lips, and said, "I think you like me?" He definitely had a German accent.

"Yes," I said.

For the first time I felt stirring in my groin.

He smiled. "My name is Fritz." Could it have been more German? "Yours?"

"Aiden."

I had an overwhelming urge to smile also.

"*Aiden*," he pronounced. I loved hearing my name come from his mouth. "Will you give me your telephone number . . ." He paused, I assumed to word the next sentence in his head before actually saying it. "We can get together sometime?" he finally said. The word *sometime* had the upward lilt that people seem to use when English is not their first language.

"I'd love that," I said.

He smiled again. "Good," he said, and nodded.

I still had not emptied my balls in preparation for David.

— 3 —

I watched, utterly captivated, as *Pink Narcissus* played on one of the largest screens in London. The film was intense. I marveled at the mind of the anonymous filmmaker who had created such a thing.

Amid a nonlinear plot, without training necessarily but with a lot of skill, Bobby Kendall, a divinely pretty model/actor with big lips and pale skin all over his body, stood, walked, or did other simple things in front of the camera in different costumes: dressed as a toreador; in an ancient Greek-style tunic; shirtless in a pair of white, almost transparent trousers and cowboy boots. Bobby unbuttoned his trousers. The fabric coated him from his waist to his ankles. Soft, sheer, erotic, it created a layer of something more perfect than mere skin on Bobby. You could actually see the indentation of the crack of his bum. His dick was clearly visible, with a bulge outlining the head. It fell heavily to his left. The camera cut to a close-up of his crotch. On the huge screen Bobby's dick looked massive—ten, twenty, at times thirty feet long. I'm not a size queen but this wasn't an unpleasant surprise on a first date.

Oh, right, Bobby was not my date. I was so lost in the movie, sometimes I forgot that David was beside me. Some might think me a jerk because of this, if I had so little shame as to tell anybody, but they'd have to see *Pink Narcissus* before condemning me. Bobby was irresistible. I must remember to warn people never to go see this film on a first date—or on any date, for that matter. It wasn't fair to your partner. He didn't stand a chance of getting attention.

How amazing to be captured on film for all time, to have thousands and thousands of men (and some women) fantasizing about you, keeping you alive in their memories, becoming a part of their subconscious. Hollywood actors never managed to get so deep inside me. My sexuality and sex drive were integral to who

I was. Like eating, safety, and comfort, sex was one of the driving forces in my life, which was probably why it was also my job.

David put his hand on my leg and quickly moved it up to my crotch. My dick was as stiff as could be. I felt a second date coming on. When the film had finished I was hot and flushed.

David and I walked to the tube, where as planned I told him I had to meet some friends. We arranged to speak on the phone. Being so worked up, I didn't want to go home. I caught the tube to Leicester Square, to the Compton Arms, and after that went to Heaven.

Shortly after I arrived, Trev the drug dealer approached me.

"I hoped you'd be here, Aiden. I wonder if you'd do me a favor."

I felt like I owed him one. "Depends what it is," I said.

He laughed. "Seriously," he said.

"I *was* being serious."

He did his laugh thing again. "You weirdo," he said. He looked around himself, wary. "Just kidding! Listen, I can't be caught with E and money on me. The police would know I sell them. That's why I get other people to handle them."

"Sorry, Trev, I'm not going to do that."

"I'm not asking you to." He looked at me with what he must have thought was sincerity. "I wouldn't do that. The thing is, I think I'm being watched. I know it sounds crazy but I think they're onto me."

"Then why are you still here?"

"People are relying on me," he said. "And it's my job. I've got to earn a living."

He shrugged his shoulders; although unintended, he appeared comical. He looked around himself again. Suddenly the music seemed louder, the club much busier. I'd be surprised if anybody could keep track of him there tonight. On second thought, I never had any trouble finding him—lately he seemed to pop up everywhere. I couldn't put my finger on what I found so creepy about him. Was it his weird facial expressions that made me think spooky stuff went on in his head? It was as though each of his thoughts was a non sequitur, and a surprise to him. He held his body as if something had gone wrong for him on the evolutionary road—something that really shouldn't have happened. I think the creepiest thing about him was the volume of his breathing. But how could I hear it over the music? Likely it was my imagination, fueled by the drugs I'd taken. The important thing was that something must have caused me to believe it.

"Anyway," he said, "I can't go home yet. I just got a shitload of gear in and I have to move it."

The truth at last.

"So what I was wondering . . ."

How much longer was this going to take?

". . . if you'd look after some cash for me."

My ears heard the words and my brain understood what they meant, but it took a few seconds to register and make sense. This was one of the more unusual things I'd been asked to do in quite a while.

"How much is there?" I asked, as though the amount would figure in my decision-making process. Still, I couldn't help being curious.

"I don't know. Not a lot. A few hundred."

In my head I tried to work out the legality of carrying his money. I often had hundreds of pounds of my own money in my pocket, but was carrying Trev's committing a crime? If somebody searched me, how would they know it wasn't mine?

My expression must have indicated agreement to his request. Like a parody of a secret agent he said, "Follow me, Aiden." He led me to a corner created by a cigarette machine and the wall near one of the archways. "Stay still," he commanded, and stuffed a fat wad of notes in my pocket.

"How much is there?"

He looked at me as though I were stupid. "I didn't count it."

"But you put it in the pocket where I keep my money."

"So?"

"I don't know how much was in there already."

"I'm not worried. I trust you. I'll find you later and give you more."

"But . . ."

"And here, have these." In the dim light he passed me what I guessed were about ten to fifteen pills, then moved off into the crowd before I had time to respond.

I felt I should get rid of the pills as soon as possible. Like Trev I didn't want to be caught with money *and* drugs on my person. I usually had large amounts of cash and drugs on me when in a nightclub, but it seemed different now that I knew the drugs and money were connected. Prostitution may have been illegal in the eyes of the law but it didn't feel like it, whereas everything about drugs did. It took Trev to make me think like a criminal. Confused, I thought, *First things first. Get a strong drink then lose the pills.* The quickest and most sensible way to get rid of pills was to swallow them.

At the bar I fiddled in my pocket and extracted one note so as not to pull out the whole wad. It was fifty pounds.

The barman rolled his eyes. "You sure you don't have anything smaller?" he asked. The idiot didn't know how to work a tip.

"Certain," I answered.

Once I had my drink I swallowed a couple of the pills. Sitting alone in one of the dimly lit arches I tried to process what had happened, at the same time waiting for the E to kick in. Things would make more sense then. Rather, I wouldn't mind what decision I came to—if I came to one at all. In about fifteen minutes I felt more ready to socialize.

I headed for the toilet. I half fell in, landing against a sweet, fair-headed, tall young thing to whom I instantly apologized.

"Sorry, lovely," I said, trying to keep macho and sexy.

"Not to worry, babe." I thought I detected an Aussie accent. "You buxom bloke."

I laughed. "Buxom sounds a bit ladylike."

"And that's a good thing, right?"

The slightly girly boy reminded me of myself ten years earlier. "I think you might have meant young buck, not buxom bloke," I said.

"Oh, how you say? Me no speak no English so good, yes?"

She, as I now thought of him, was clearly having fun but not at my expense. Joking with her further, I said, "What'd you say your name wuz? Sheila?"

"Close, you wingy pom," she said, running with it. "Actually it's Heidi."

She was definitely an Aussie. I pressed five or six E's into her hand.

"Hey, Heidi. See how delicious you feel on these. They're called Love Doves, baby."

"You darlin'!" she said, realizing what was happening. She made a delighted, young, innocent and girlish, surprised face that over the years I came to know as her signature expression. "What do I owe you for these?"

"Just stay delicious."

With the enthusiasm of a child she said, "My name's Heidi Licious, then."

"I'm liking that name, Miss Licious."

"*Ms.* Licious, if you don't mind." A cubicle came free. "You first, doll. I'm a modern Ms. Licious."

Like a very modern gentleman, I went before her. Heidi gave me a sweet, darling, genuine smile—at least it seemed like that in my drug haze—and a good feeling inside. I felt I'd made a friend for life. That's how E works. After doing some coke I walked out of the cubicle less clumsily than I'd fallen in.

There were bound to be at least one or two, if not most of the Burlington boys at Heaven at the beginning of the weekend. Kydd and S were the first I came across. I unloaded the last two pills on them. They both tried to pay me but gave in easily when I wouldn't let them. We all had plenty of money and were always generous with each other. Money meant very little to us, which was odd considering what we had to do to earn it. We had so much of it and there was always more coming, so we spent it. I don't think any of us ever thought to save any.

It happened to be Heaven's birthday party, or something of the sort (it didn't take much to get people clubbing), and many famous people had turned out. Neil Tennant from the Pet Shop Boys was there, as were Marc Almond from Soft Cell, Andy Bell and Vince Clarke from Erasure, George Michael from Wham!, Siouxsie Sue from Siouxsie and the Banshees, a few members of Sigue Sigue Sputnik, and some Gay TV people, all too tedious and embarrassing to mention.

In addition to these well-known figures were some of the *real* stars of London. Freaks like drag monster Sheila Tequila and Bodymap fashion designer David Holah. The video/film director John Maybury was with his model boyfriend Baillie Walsh. Spinning in his special stardust scattered solar system was Space. Michael Hardy, the opera-loving skinhead muscleman. Choreographer/dancer Les Child was oozing love from every one of her minute and possibly makeup-covered pores. Miss Kimberly was fresh, a new boy in town who spoke of runways in New York and was beautifully reinventing herself. Living eyesore (in the best possible way) art/fashion thingamajig Leigh Bowery was with his sober-in-comparison good friend Fat Jill. The lovable and ever snoglicious Jeffrey Hinton was DJ, along with Tallulah and style icon Princess Julia. Steve Strange from Visage, and Philip Salon and Boy George's Marilyn were also present (Boy himself was nowhere to be seen). Most of these I knew to some degree or other, some not as well as I would have liked to, others too well for comfort. And of course there were those I ducked for cover from for fear of being spotted. Regardless of my likes or dislikes, as far as I was concerned these creatures were what gave London its edge and made it a tourist destination (at least for Japanese club kids). You could fuck the Queen (*yeuuw*) or Big Ben (ouch!).

As Trev promised, he gave me another wad of money later, again stuffing it in my pocket. By then I was too high to worry about trying to keep track of how much money there was and which was mine. Once more he put pills into my hand. My solution was to dispense them as I did before, to S and Kydd and also to a Spaniard who'd joined our little crowd. Everyone was happy. The pills made it so. They borrowed our bodies to express themselves. We rode the E and clung on as best we could, all the while grinning, a little manically at times.

Before the club shut down for the night Trev repeated his transfers a final time and said he'd pop around to my place the next day to collect the money. Somehow I ended up back at my flat alone on E.

It wasn't until I closed the door that I realized the severity of my situation. Silly me, I'd been too high to plan otherwise. I was stuck. There'd be nowhere open now. Every club in London closed at two o'clock. I felt too happy to phone a chat line, so there was little else I could do but resort to sleeping tablets and jerking off.

The mix I preferred when wanking was part sweet thoughts,

beautiful memories, and imagination. Bobby Kendall rode my dick, climbing off only so I could lick his bum, all while wearing his gauze-like trousers. Kydd cut in, or maybe it was more a slow dissolve. Anyway, he wore his faded green shorts, had my balls in his mouth, and looked up at me. Gary, the gym trainer from the Burlington, lay on his stomach with his silky smooth hairy bum before me. I drove my tongue deep inside him. Terry made an appearance but now wasn't the time or place for ideas about men I liked so much, and I moved on. The American jackass Love came to mind for a moment, but was easily dislodged. Regardless, it was all prime viewing and it was hard to focus on any body or body part in particular. Sensations streamed into my head, textured, sensual, and textural. Some were motionless, caught in their finest moment, others moved and I was able to occupy them, become part of them. It was unfair to call them images. They were more like experiences cramming, wrestling, and bucking for attention. Nobody got hurt, manhandled, or was any the wiser for me using them this way. David appeared amid a crowd scene. It was all getting a bit blurry.

In the end the ultimate star of my extravaganza was Fritz, my boy from the YMCA showers. I was licking his bum and simultaneously kissing him, physically impossible but it made sense. Finally I came up Fritz's bum. I passed out before being able to clean up my mess.

Saturday

I WOKE TO LOUD KNOCKING ON MY FRONT DOOR. Confused, hazy, still under the influence of sleeping tablets, I lumbered clumsily out of bed naked and cursed as I knocked over a cup of water. This was directed at the cup, myself, and whoever was knocking on the door. At least it wasn't coffee or anything containing soured milk. For some reason, last night I'd thought it okay to leave an unwrapped Mars bar on the hallway floor, near a radiator. Although the softened candy felt kind of nice between my toes, it still annoyed me.

"Hello?" I called out at the front door, my voice phlegm-filled and croaking.

"Hello," whoever was on the other side stupidly replied.

Kennington wasn't a safe enough area for me to trustingly open the door. "Who is it?" I demanded as impatiently as possible on downers. Such feelings weren't at my disposal yet.

"Trev," he said as though it was the most obvious thing in the world.

I'd forgotten that he said he'd come around to collect the money.

I positioned myself behind the door as I opened it. Trev stood there bug-eyed, accompanied by the weird smell from yesterday morning. I told myself they couldn't be connected, it was simply the first time I'd let "fresh" air into my flat today. We looked vacantly at each other, him with a less than subtle grinding of his jaw, me dopey from downers.

"Well!" he said like an exasperated teenager. "Aren't you going to invite me in?"

Inviting Trev into my home had not crossed my mind. My inclination was to deal with him at the door.

"Let me grab some shorts," I said, closing the door but not shutting it completely. I didn't want to be rude.

The first thing that came to hand in the drawer under my bed was a pair of snug boxer shorts with a stars-and-stripes design. *I must throw out my horrible old clothes*, I thought. Then I checked myself: *Take them to a thrift shop.*

When I got back to the door it was slightly open. I'd been living in my flat long enough to know this doesn't happen by itself. A draft would have caused it to shut. I felt a little creeped out, which was the feeling I generally had around Trev when I wasn't high. Maybe that's why he helped induce this state in me. I didn't ask him how he knew which number I lived at. He must have counted the floors from his window and worked out which apartment would be mine. It wouldn't be that difficult. There were only four on each floor, one at each corner.

Trev stepped into my hallway and looked around. "Wow!" he said, and paused. "Crazy place."

Despite my fuzzy vision and even fuzzier brain, I sensed it wasn't the spectacle that I'd created with the layer of varnished oak leaves lining the walls that surprised him. More likely it had something to do with me having less clothes on than usual.

"I guess I'm a *crazy* kid," I said.

"You crack me up," he said without conviction. He looked me

over. His mouth twitched. "You're in great shape," he said, his roving eyes covertly taking in my crotch. "You must work out every day."

Even though I had boxers on, Trev made me feel naked.

"There's a gym at work. When it's not busy we tend to mess around with the weights, out of boredom more than anything."

His eyes fell to my stomach. "Been eating custard in bed?"

I looked down at the large smear of dried cum. "You got it," I said, lifting my hand to cover it.

To my relief he broke the awkward silence. "The money."

"Of course," I said.

I walked into my bedroom to get my jeans, neglecting to tell Trev to wait where he was. I turned to find him in the doorway looking at my bed. I attempted to show surprise, finding it difficult to express *What the fuck are you doing?* subtly. Jeans in hand, I led him back into the hall, determined not to let him intrude into any more of my private space. He'd already been in my kitchen, how many times I couldn't bear to imagine.

I pulled all the money out of the jeans pocket.

"Looks like a good night," he said with a little laugh.

"My money's mixed in with that."

"Still. How much did you have?" He looked to his left. It's said that when someone looks to the right they're trying to access memory and when looking to their left they're creating a lie. "Five hundred?"

I guessed he was making up a figure but intended to err in my favor so I'd end up with more money. I was happy to go with his estimate.

"About that much, give or take a punter," I said.

"You're a scream," he said. "Take out five for yourself and something extra. Eighty pounds sound okay?"

Eighty seemed an arbitrary amount but was all right. I'd

bought endless drinks for myself and everybody with me, as well as being given loads of free E. But I wanted him to understand I'd done him a favor and we were even now.

I shrugged.

"Good. Give me the rest."

I counted the money and got him out of the flat relatively easily. Maybe he thought he had no excuse to be there anymore. Whatever the reason, I was glad to have him gone.

I felt even better once I was back in bed. It was important that I get plenty of sleep today. I was starting at ten tomorrow morning and it was a long shift. I wanted to be fresh; otherwise it would be too difficult. To speed sleep along and generally aid my recovery I took more drugs, pharmaceutical grade downers. Technically they weren't recreational, even if I didn't use them as intended by doctors.

I jerked off again but this time didn't mess around with random visuals that came to mind. I went straight to Fritz, the source of all beauty. He told me he loved me. I came in about two minutes.

Sunday

An unusually scrubbed-up Cubus stood behind the reception desk wearing a white shirt, his hair gelled down to one side.

"Cubus!" I said, surprised at his imitation of proper, and burst out laughing.

"Hello," he said frostily.

"Are you okay?" I said.

"*I'm* okay, but you're ten minutes late."

"Yeah, the tube . . ." I started to explain.

"I want to hear this." His expression was unfamiliar, alien.

"Why, what concern is it of yours? Anyway, what are you doing behind the desk?"

"I've been promoted."

"What!" Who would consider doing the desk at a glorified brothel a promotion?

"Why so surprised?"

So many reasons flashed through my mind—*because you never come to work, you're a junky, you have no experience, you can't be trusted with money.*

"I don't know," I said, still baffled. "Was that Sandy's idea?"

"Sandy's gone. He got the sack."

A rush of chemicals surged through my body, which seemed strange because I hadn't taken any drugs since yesterday morning. My brain was doing it of its own accord. Legend had it that when Sandy was a teenager he'd been cute. Apparently he'd been kept by one of the Burlington's four owners and loaned out to the others whenever they felt like it. The rumor was he'd give them all blowjobs free of charge. All of these gents were over sixty, and they all insisted he took their cum in his mouth and swallowed. Three of them were married. After a few years his sugar daddy found someone younger and Sandy was given a job as a masseur at the Burlington. But nobody ever hired him; all he did was pick up towels, make tea, and clean the showers. Back then the minimum was ten pounds per shift. Sandy's former sugar daddy took pity and gave him a job on reception. That was over ten years ago.

Some people think that being a kept boy is an easy life. However, I knew which owner it was and his severe halitosis alone must have made Sandy's life unbearable. His résumé would read: hustled on the street as a teenager, kept boy until he lost his looks, brothel desk clerk for five years. Poor, poor Sandy.

"Why did they sack him?" I asked Cubus.

"That's none of your concern."

"What's with the attitude, you freak?"

"Don't talk to me like that. This is your first warning. You have two more, then I sack you."

"Freak!"

"One more and you're back on the street. I mean it."

I looked him in the eye and said, "Sorry."

He smirked.

"What I meant to say was, *fucking* freak!"

"Clear out your locker and get out of here."

"What are you going to do, call the police? I'd like to see how that affects business."

"You can hang out here all you like, for all I care. You're not getting any bookings off me and you won't be paid for shifts."

"You're insane."

"Maybe, but I have the power to sack you, loser."

With surprising calm I went to the kitchen and spoke with S and Kydd. This was more about annoying Cubus, as I could have called both of them at home later. Next I wrote out my home telephone number and gave it to several of my favorite customers. Then I cleared out my locker. All this with Cubus watching from a safe distance. He knew not to get too close.

Upstairs, Sleeve greeted me warmly. He hadn't been on the door when I arrived, as he'd also been late. He shook his head then opened his arms in a fatherly way as I approached him.

"Cubus told me he was going to get rid of you today. I thought he'd wait until later."

"He already knew?"

"She told me on the phone last night. The power went to her head."

"Listen, I want to get out of here. Let's talk on the phone."

Sleeve gave me a hug. "Talk to you later."

It was a relief to get outside. I started to walk down Old Bond Street towards the tube but stopped and stared into space, pretending to look in a shop window. It was too soon to make sense of my situation. Distraction was in order. If ever there was a good reason to drink alcohol before lunchtime it was right now. The Compton Arms seemed the obvious place to do it. I turned around and headed towards Soho.

The Compton Arms was just opening. I was the first customer. The landlord, Dolly (named after his drag persona, Ms. Parton), raised his eyebrows as if in surprise. Then he said the opposite.

"I guess it doesn't surprise me."

"It's been a rough day," I said seriously.

"Bloody hell," he said, having never lost the slightest bit of the only masculine thing about him, his Mancunian accent. "I'm all ears."

Dolly liked to think of himself as motherly, and fell into this role easily. I wondered if he had any male roles that suited him as comfortably. I presumed not. But he must have been as bored as I was confused.

"Just between you and me . . ." I began.

I paused. My telling Dolly would mean that he'd serve the news item with every drink today. ("Ice? Slice? Gossip?") Not such a bad thing, only I might still be in the pub. If people were going to discuss me I'd rather they did it behind my back. After all, once my story got distorted into an anecdote worth repeating it tended to have little to do with truth and literally was none of my business. If told well it became rumor, which if repeated to the right queens evolved into urban legend with a life of its own. I had no problem letting it run free. As they said, "if it loved me it would return." I have heard the most fantastical gossip about myself and each time I thought, *If only my life were that exciting, fun, outrageous, and sexy*. Then again my memory wasn't so sharp when I took drugs. Some of what was said about me might be true. At worst it gave me jerk-off material.

Meanwhile Dolly wanted her scoop. It might as well be good if it was going to get such great coverage. With an exhausted sigh, I lowered my head slowly and paused for a count of three seconds. With all the gravity I could load into my act, I raised my head once more and looked in Dolly's direction, but not straight in his eyes. I positioned my line of sight slightly to his right, as though trying to summon a memory, and included a facial expression of subtle but deep torment meant to convey that I wasn't able to face the idea—or Dolly.

"Just between you and me," I said again, enjoying the absurdity, "I think I killed someone."

He couldn't have responded more perfectly. Without saying a word he swallowed. I assumed he believed my story. To add further proof I ordered vodka neat and lager, and drank it all in one. This almost made me retch but was worth it. It added a wild, hard-looking edge to my character. After a respectful but clumsy space of time in which Dolly gathered up glasses and washed ashtrays, he leaned over the bar and spoke close to my ear.

"I know you're a good kid. I'm sure you had your reasons."

He backed away and looked around to confirm that nobody was listening. Then he leaned in again, too close for my liking. I could smell cheese and onion crisps on his breath.

"This goes no further," he promised.

From then on he found reasons to avoid my side of the bar. Oddly enough, I think he meant what he said about not telling anybody else. Was this what it took to get his respect? Had I managed to tap into a nicer side of Dolly that most of his customers didn't know existed?

Throughout the day several people that I knew came into the pub. Some hung out a while and others left after a drink or two, enough to get them home to whatever waited—partners, family, loneliness. I was in for the long haul, until I decided what to do with my life. The pub would probably close before I had an epiphany about my future, but I knew by that point I wouldn't mind. One drink followed another and gradually things became clearer.

As one might expect, I wondered about finding work. More precisely, I tried to imagine how money might come to me. My résumé was as unimpressive as Sandy's. But not for one second did I consider getting a regular job. What concerned me most was the embarrassment of getting sacked from a brothel. God knows what crap Cubus would make up about me. Anybody who knew him and me would understand but I didn't like the idea of my punters thinking I'd done something dishonest or immoral.

Who would have thought being a whore would be such a safe option, so mundane and predictable, shockingly nine-to-five. A few years ago it had seemed more like joining the army, but an even queerer and sexier one—with more hard-ons and better pay. It promised travel, adventure, meeting new people (often naked), thrills, being on the front line (the street), danger, risking life on a daily basis, and servicing the nation. At the Burlington I plodded down the stairs every day knowing that I'd see a certain amount of flesh and several hard-ons. I'd use the same lines— "And will you be wanting extras?" "Do you want me to cum?" "Would you like this in your mouth?" It had become difficult to know anymore whether I'd rather they answered yes or no to any of these questions. Sexual innuendos and puns came to mind so easily and often that I used them constantly. The truth was the Burlington bored me. I was glad to be rid of it. I had plenty of money and enough regulars to keep me going for now. Fuck the Burlington. Something was bound to come up. It always did.

More than once I thought to walk around the corner to the Golden Lion and try earning some money the old way. Each time I reminded myself that it wasn't necessary, that it was more for sport than necessity, more about seeing if I *could*. Prostitution was usually associated with desperation but to me it had always felt like a choice, an interesting hobby. The more profound question was why I took it—and its effects—so lightly.

1991
The Beginning

The Clinique

THE EARLS COURT CLINIC WAS A MASSAGE PARLOR. AS THE name suggested, it was in Earls Court. Although it was spelled *clinic*, everybody pronounced it *clinique*. Nobody knew how this name came about. Possibly it was a joke by the boys, or an affectation of the eccentric owner. Either explanation was likely. The Clinique had a sleazier image than the Burlington. This may have been because the owner wasn't as choosy about who he hired. Clinique boys didn't have to speak well, be able to hold a conversation, or have nice manners. And they didn't have to be legally certified masseurs. The only qualifications required for working there were sex appeal, having some kind of "look," and being good at putting out. The Clinique tended to hire a more "street" type of boy. As a result it attracted a different, fresh batch of untapped punters. Occasionally there'd be crossovers with the Burlington, the kind of men who tried every place and anybody. Obviously these men were not looking for love and I suspect that their compulsion hadn't much to do with sex either.

The price for massages was the same at both establishments, but the Clinique didn't have the yearly membership fee. Nor did it have a sauna, steam room, or gym, or make any other pretense that it had something to do with health and fitness in the traditional sense. All this worked in the boys' favor. If a punter chose us, we knew he wanted some kind of sex. We never had to do straight massages, the bane of the Burlington boys.

The Clinique was located in a basement flat off a very ordinary road. The entrance gave away nothing about the goings-on inside. But you might begin to guess something was out of kilter once you pressed the doorbell, as an elaborate chiming would commence.

When entering a brothel with the intent on having sex with a rentboy, you had to have accepted to some degree that suspension of disbelief was already in process. But nobody in real life behaved like the Clinique's owner. Peter would answer the door with a servile, sweet, gracious manner like an actor in a racist British sitcom from the Seventies. He'd invite the punter into a room that looked like something from a Disney theme park, furnished with sofas covered in red silk. In one corner was a small, relentlessly trickling water fountain. Another corner housed a statue of the Buddha. There were many plants, all plastic. Mirrored walls gave the illusion of space, and the dim lighting was kind to all flaws and irregularities. Overall the room had a bordello meets jungle meets temple feel to it. Peter would encourage the punter to sit, and offer him tea or coffee. Only after he had refused was the punter finally escorted down the hallway to the TV room to see the delights on show that particular day.

When the doorbell chimed, all the boys straightened up, got in position, pulled off their T-shirts, or set about doing whatever their trick was to look as desirable as possible. Unlike at the Burlington, the Clinique boys sat in a room watching TV or doing whatever we were able to in such a noisy, smoky environment. One of us would close the door and shortly afterwards Peter would tap on the two-way inset mirror to let us know that a punter was looking at us. If the punter had difficulty choosing, Peter would point him in the right direction by telling him who had what size dick and who would or wouldn't do certain things. Once he'd picked his prey, the punter was sent into one of three massage rooms to undress and wait while Peter popped his head into the TV room and told us who the lucky boy was.

Some of the boys thought Peter's eccentricity bordered on insanity. I thought he was simply unusual. He was from Thailand and English was his second language. But he was able to run a successful business and keep the police off his back, all while saving a fortune. He owned the flat that he'd converted into the Clinique, and although he was forced to close several times due to neighbors' complaints about him being undesirable, he always managed to reopen. More than any other working boy in London I probably got to know him best. He confided to me that he bribed the police, and showed me photos of his huge house and grounds back in Thailand.

Despite my dissatisfaction with the Burlington, the convenience factor made me go over to the Clinique. And it didn't hurt that they were the Burlington's competition. Besides, the Clinique had an edge that was totally lacking at the Burlington. When I first interviewed at the Clinique, Peter asked me to give him a massage. This didn't seem that unusual to me. Only later did I hear that nobody else had "auditioned" in this way. Whatever I did must have impressed Peter; on a weekly basis, when the place was quiet often he'd call me in for a massage. So as not to be found out, he'd ring the front doorbell himself then knock on the two-way mirror as usual. I never knew it was him until I got inside the massage room. As a punter he was undemanding and only ever wanted to suck me off. He asked me not to tell the other boys and I didn't. But the other boys could tell I was his favorite. Around me Peter would become coy, smiling, and bashful, whereas with the other boys he was icy and weary, a strange mix. If a boy annoyed him Peter's ability to speak or hear things in English diminished entirely. Consequently he began to depend on me. More often he'd ask me to deal with people he didn't want to.

Initially I'd take the telephone if Peter couldn't understand what somebody was saying to him. This led to him asking me to deal with a customer he didn't like, or to watch the desk while he took a nap. Eventually Peter hardly ever came out of his room. My guess was he was depressed, lonely, and simply not enjoying his life. How could he? I don't remember him ever leaving the basement. He had everything he needed brought to him. Some might think this luxurious. I saw it as a self-imposed prison. He found the outside world threatening, loud, ugly—everything he tried so hard to avoid in the version of reality he'd created in the Clinique.

Finally he left the greeting of punters to me. Being less strange for them, I believe this encouraged business. There was no doubt it was also good for me. As a punter entered I interacted with him. From my days at the Burlington, I was well-versed in making myself seem sexy, horny, a nice guy. By the time the punter looked through the two-way mirror it was often a mere formality, because his crotch already had told him whom to choose. The boys sitting in the TV room might as well have been two-dimensional figures. Some of them didn't even have the sense to move or interact with another boy. They just stared moronically at the TV. Had I been choosing, I wouldn't think they'd be much fun in the massage room. Often the punter would turn to me and surreptitiously ask if I ever did massages. Unlike the desk staff at the Burlington, I did. This must have made some of the other boys resent me but anybody who'd worked at the Clinique a while knew that I always got booked a lot, whether I was on the desk or not.

Within six months I was running the place. This included ordering and paying for things like the laundry service, keeping track of stock (everything from coffee to condoms), plus incidentals like handling the cable TV bill and water rates. It was all becoming far too much like a real job for me again. Something had to give.

David and Hugo and Timmy and Cubus

DAVID AND I AFFECTIONATELY REFERRED TO OUR FIRST date as individual dates with the film *Pink Narcissus*. We just happened to have gone to the same showing, sat together, and left at the same time. Otherwise we were with Bobby Kendall. That had been over a year ago and it didn't deter us. I found David adorable, clever, and odd, exactly the kind of mix that attracted me. He has since admitted that he'd wanted my dick up his bum. True love runs the most unusual path, or should I say gays are predictable when it comes to big dicks.

We had a more successful second date, a dinner where we realized that we liked each other followed by sex in which our physical chemistry made all the dogs in South London howl in recognition. After that I didn't hear from him for a few days and began to wonder if I'd done something wrong. Maybe he had been pretending to laugh at my jokes or thinking about somebody else while I fucked him. I thought I'd done a fair job sexually—after all, I was a pro. The problem was that I wasn't a professional comic and people's sense of humor varied much more than the generally accepted view of what good sex was. So even if I'd excelled in bed, David could still consider me a complete idiot.

When he did finally call, I felt relieved. But shock quickly replaced this. With a trembling voice, he said, "Aiden," and immediately started to cry.

"Hey! What's wrong?"

This wasn't the kind of question for which I expected a clear, thought-out, rational verbal response. I waited while he sobbed.

In time, he said, "I tried to kill myself."

It's not that the gravity of David's situation was lost on me, but Terry immediately sprang into my mind. I pictured his sticking-up, caramel-color hair, his little red nose, and the milky smell of his pale skin. Several months after his initial attempt to kill himself, Terry finally succeeded. Somebody told me the news in Heaven while I was high. Terry's mother had been looking after him, keeping him out of harm's way. I'd had no way of contacting him. Why he didn't call me I'll never know. Apparently he'd gone to bed as normal one night, swallowed a lethal amount of downers, and left the window open. Once he'd passed out he died of hypothermia. Obviously this time he was determined to end his life. It broke my heart. I felt that pain all over again with David now.

"I'm coming to get you," I told him.

He didn't protest or even ask what I meant. There was no need for an explanation. When I got to his flat we collected some of his stuff in a big sports bag and got a cab all the way back to mine. David wasn't concerned about leaving his place, and explained that the other people in the house were merely roommates, not friends. A week later his father's chauffeur dropped off the rest of his belongings. The move was official. I have to admit that I got a kick out of seeing his father's elegant black Mercedes at the entrance to my squalid council tower block. For David this new life was very different from his highly privileged upbringing. Possibly this meant he must have really liked me. That or he was desperate, and after attempting suicide and not succeeding, I was his last resort. Maybe not so flattering after all.

We couldn't have been more different. David had been educated at boarding school then gone to Cambridge for his BA and MA in natural sciences (specializing in microbiology). My education would have embarrassed a tinker. David was well-spoken, sat up straight, and had the correct answer to any question I threw at him. I mumbled, muttered, and didn't enunciate, in part due to me lacking confidence about what I was saying. I believed I could barely form a question, let alone answer one. I didn't know what a noun was or how a sentence could be made passive. Sentences had sexual preferences? When it came to posture I could no more sit up straight than have straight sex. David was mature, patient, and accepted my peculiarities. In comparison I was like a lamb, as wobbly on my legs, as hungry, bleating, and woolly. Despite these differences, our interaction was effortless—no ego issues, no macho power games, no weird dynamics. We settled into being boyfriends seamlessly.

About three months later Hugo came to stay with us.

Hugo and I had been boyfriends when I was about nineteen. Our relationship had worked quite well, with relatively little drama. This might have been because I was his first boyfriend and so he accepted my odd character, having nothing to compare me to. Hugo was tall, fit, and blond, with James Dean good looks, but he carried himself in an apologetic way, which made him much more beautiful to me. Even at that age I liked a broken edge to my men, maybe because they cut, made me feel. The lack of drama in our relationship might have had something to do with Hugo's family life. After the carefree summer we spent together, his father killed himself, using the exhaust in his car. Hugo inherited the car and believed he could always smell the fumes. My memories of that car were sweet. On long drives I used to give him blowjobs while he was at the wheel. It was reckless but he assured me he could keep control of the car while having an orgasm. (Of course, he *would* say that.) I didn't care to argue the point. I had no room to talk. After all, I couldn't drive—and my mouth was full.

A more constant concern for Hugo was his mother, who was manic-depressive. I'd spent time with her during one of her depressive phases and found her eyes like a black hole I feared being sucked into. In reality when Hugo's mother was depressed she couldn't be bothered with anyone, if she was even aware of their presence. Strangely, there was something morbidly seductive about her inertia and her lack of interest in interacting with anything around her. Hugo grew up in a different world than most of us, one in which the concept of *fair* simply didn't apply.

After living in France for a couple of years he had moved to London in 1989. It seemed natural that he and I should want to spend time together when he got there, but without the blinding vision of infatuation our differences were much more apparent and we didn't. But during his time abroad he'd grown into a man, with hairy forearms and a mature, comfortable-in-his-skin knowingness. Moreover, he had a French lilt to his voice. Normally this would make me want to puke but on Hugo it worked. He still turned me on. Hugo and I also still had an emotional connection and within a matter of weeks of his moving in our relationship reverted to what it had been years before.

What surprised all three of us was that this time David was included. It started as sex after we'd had a few drinks. In time we all became romantically involved. The relationship had a basic core: David and I were boyfriends and Hugo shared our setup. Technically he was just staying with us for a while. None of us saw his inclusion as a permanent thing. After a complex yet simplistic day of having my dick sucked for money I'd go home to an even more complex but usually more satisfying evening with David and Hugo. The math of our varying psychologies, backgrounds, and educations didn't add up but it served its purpose.

One day Hugo woke me excitedly, urging me to look at the front page of *The News of the World*. The headline read GENTLEMEN'S HEALTH CLUB COVER FOR A MALE BROTHEL. The Burlington had been busted by the Vice Squad. It was a funny article with even funnier photos of Timmy and Cubus leaving the place attempting to cover their faces with their hands. I'd heard that Timmy and Cubus were also in a three-way relationship—the two of them with heroin. S told me that Timmy got Sandy sacked so that Cubus and he could run the Burlington and steal from the register to pay for their habit. They had a fancy, expensive flat off Piccadilly. It turned out I had been right about timid Timmy having a dark side.

Lionel and Brian

LIONEL LOOKED ME IN THE EYE, STEADY AND KEEN. "So what time is he coming?" he said.

"I told him seven."

"It's seven now."

"I know. He'll show. He's a good kid."

I purposely used the word *kid* to imply youth.

Lionel had become my favorite punter. He was warm and had what felt like real affection for me. He made me believe I was liked, special, and wanted. After meeting with him a few times he started to ask me about other boys. One of the first things he'd want to know was their age. It wasn't long before I realized that the younger they were the more excited he appeared. It became my job to bring new boys to him. I'd always tell him they were fourteen. If I wanted to drive him nuts I'd purposely be vague, as though I didn't dare say how young they really were. In fact I never introduced him to anybody under eighteen and who wasn't already working as a rentboy. The legal age of consent for gay sex in Britain was twenty-one. This seemed not just absurd but prejudiced. No doubt much younger boys had sex with other much younger boys, but personally I felt that as soon as somebody older was involved an imbalance of power was likely to occur. Balance is rare even in most "normal" relationships, which perhaps is not surprising when you take into account that the majority of couples are of different sexes. It's even said that power—of a man over a woman—can be an aphrodisiac. Suspicious as I am, I find it difficult not to wonder exactly who propagates these myths. I was willing to believe that older/younger relationships could also work, be advantageous to both parties, and even lead to happiness. Knowing this, how could anybody begin to have a moral benchmark, let alone a standpoint? There are too many variants and I believe most of them are completely biased. But my gut feeling was that once money was introduced into the equation the result could only be harmful. Unsurprisingly this is not only accepted but prevalent in heterosexual relationships. Oddly enough it always has been.

My beeper vibrated against my stomach. Before I even looked to see who it was, I acknowledged that I felt impressed that life had become so modern. Now somebody could page me with a message or their number, and I'd call them back. Gone were the days of having to wait at home in case I got a telephone call. Some things in this modern world seemed pure evil, like germ warfare or the Pope, but a pager so that a punter horny for boy meat could get a message to me anywhere in London—actually in the whole of England—well, that seemed like a gift from God.

It was from Brian. Just in case I had to edit the message, I read it to myself first and only then aloud: *Sorry. I'll be there in fifteen minutes.*

"I guess we should have a drink," said Lionel.

"Sounds good to me."

Lionel stood up slowly and shuffled to a cabinet at the far end of his large sitting room. I was used to this sight; each time I saw him, at some point a drink would be in order.

"I've been thinking more about your screenplay," he said. "What do think of Yoko Ono playing Eve?"

Surprised and at the same time unimpressed, I said, "Once out of Eden, the actress who plays Eve changes in every scene."

Lionel turned to me. "Yeah, but I was thinking the original Eve," he said with the seriousness he always used when it came to something work-oriented. "In paradise, before she becomes more real."

"I hear you. I like that she's Japanese. But ideally I'd like somebody whose ethnicity was more ambiguous, more exotic."

"I read that in the script. I just thought it would be cool to have a name like hers attached to this."

Poor Lionel was so out of touch.

"I could call her right now."

"It's tempting," I said, finding him amusing. "I think it makes more sense to have unknown actors. It's easier for the audience to suspend disbelief."

Lionel raised his eyebrows in surprise. "Very good! Clever."

"And *you're* very kind."

I'd worked out every detail of *Would You Adam and Eve It* long ago—the art direction, type of film (super eight), and the exact look of the actors I wanted to use.

With a drink in each hand Lionel made his way back to me, his steps slow, with an almost imperceptible pause between footfalls. It was obvious he was thinking intensely.

"It struck me how you've managed to write something both homoerotic and feminist," he said.

"Maybe a little too much of both. Possibly too heavy-handed?"

He passed me my drink. "No, you got the balance right." He paused. "But clear this up for me. In Eden Adam is mixed race, but once outside paradise this actor is white and stays the same in each scene while Eve changes?"

"It's meant to indicate a white supremacist notion that men

are fundamentally 'correct' while women are constantly attempting to fit into a trend or fashion or body type. It's like she is never right and so keeps changing."

"My goodness, Aiden. On exactly how many levels does this film work?"

"To five decimal places it would be roughly three point one four one five nine."

He got the joke and shook his head, then punctuated it (as he did most things) with a swig of whiskey and sat down. I went and crouched in front of him.

"I really appreciate you taking an interest in it."

He laughed. "I wouldn't if it wasn't good, Aiden." Then he winked and said, "I'm simply not that nice."

"I know you like to think you're a bit of a bad boy, but you're not really. You're very lovable"

Squinting, he looked down. "I *was*."

"No, you *are*."

"Only because I pay for it."

"You pay for *sex*, not to be *liked*. You can't help that. It just happens."

"You're a charmer, Aiden."

"I'm just honest."

Lionel swirled his drink around in his glass. "I've had a great life," he said. He changed his train of thought abruptly, and with it his mood. "The thing I like best about your script is the idea that reality is better than the more idealized Eden. Because doubt, fear, pain, hunger, and everything else that came with not being in paradise is the stuff that makes life so rich."

"Something tells me you'd prefer Eden."

He looked into space dreamily. A naughty grin spread across his face. "You're probably right. I don't mind perfection."

"Even the bland, synthetic one I created in Eden?"

"I do like glittering fruit, AstroTurf, and studio lighting more than speckled bananas, overgrown grass, and . . ." He shuddered. "Daylight."

"But you also like realness. That's why I think you'll like young Brian."

As if on cue the buzzer sounded.

"Lionel, do yourself a favor and don't subject him to the intercom. Just buzz him straight in."

"Good thinking. It is a bit scary."

"A bit?"

Jumping to my feet I said, "Actually, I'll get it." I pressed the door release before Lionel could object. "I'll open it too." I looked back at Lionel wondering about what first impression he'd make. "Oy!" I said, "Do up your dressing gown and pull in your tummy a bit."

With a splutter, he burst out laughing. Whiskey dripped down his face. "Ah, Aiden," he cackled, shaking his head and rubbing his chin with the back of his hand and finally wiping it on his dressing gown. "You kill me!"

As I turned towards the door, out of the corner of my eye I saw him set about addressing both of my suggestions.

Brian leapt up the stairs in about four bounds and appeared— panting, fresh-faced, his hair tousled and hanging down under his cap in long strands over his eyes and nose.

"Hey, beauty," I said.

I was about to straighten his cap before presenting him to Lionel but stopped. Lionel would love the cap cocked to one side like a naughty schoolboy's. Brian fitted exactly the fantasy of Lionel's ideal boy.

I noticed Lionel's jaw drop a little when he saw Brian, but he quickly turned it into a small yawn.

"Maybe you should have had the nap after all," I said, to back up the visual.

"Nah, I'm good."

It seems relevant to mention here that I had, not so much an infatuation with as massive aesthetic appreciation for Brian. Idealized he was not, but he *was* perfect. Brian looked as though he was about to come into flower. Although I wasn't confident the bloom would be anywhere near as perfect as the bud, for now he was just right. Neither tall nor fit, he went against current ideas of what was beautiful. He was on the skinny side, with scraggly, boyish hair and extremely pale skin. This might have been due to illness. Selfishly I never thought to ask him, because I loved how he looked. He had big, dry, slightly purple lips and eyes that were an odd, light tan color. Despite his boyish appearance there was an undeniable element of the "street" about Brian, a dangerous quality that no amount of washing and styling could remove. On seeing him, most women would have tucked their handbags tight against them. Other "good" people would have shuddered and thought, *There but for the grace of God go I.* Lionel and I, and other odd birds like us, simply sighed and swooned. Brian fit perfectly my idea of what my character Adam should look like, post-paradise.

"You must be Lionel," he said.

"And you must be the delightful Brian."

"Did *he* call me delightful?" Brian said with the cheek I adore him for, gesturing towards me.

Lionel leaned forward to shake Brian's hand. "No! No! No! That was my wording."

"Cause he is a funny bugger," Brian said, winking at me and blowing me a gruff kiss.

He looked at his watch and undid the cord of his tracksuit bottoms. My dick shifted in my boxers, pulsing with blood.

"Steady on, Brian," said Lionel. "Believe me, I want to get in there more than you could imagine but do you want to give an old man a heart attack?"

"Aiden's not an old man, he's only . . . oh, I don't know . . ."

At this point many a boy might have been cruel and said I was thirty or even forty, but Brian opted for charm.

". . . in his early twenties?"

Everything Brian did had so much character. In a film he might have come across as too much but in reality he was just the right amount, in a little-too-much kind of way.

"Twenty-*three*!" I added, a little too defensively.

A smile almost split Brian's face in two and his eyes sparkled like Christmas tree lights. Phew! He was comfortable and taking to Lionel. Obviously, in a situation such as this it could go either way. I wanted them to like each other but not so much that Lionel would replace me. My gut feeling was that Lionel liked a steady, fresh supply of boys, and he knew I could keep them coming. I worked in a brothel with new boys turning up all the time and I had my fingers in many pies. It wasn't always easy to find boys that looked as young as Lionel liked, but a well-intended lie goes a long way in somebody's fantasy.

Lionel clasped his hands together. "I think a drink's in order," he said.

"Do you have any lemonade?" said Brian with the enthusiasm of a kid in a TV ad.

I could see Lionel's knees go weak. Luckily I was sitting down, so physically it didn't matter that mine did. Brian's seamless rendition of like-me-or-lump-me had always seemed to turn sentient, usually intelligent men into mindless, crotch-driven, servile fools.

"We sure do," said Lionel, now in the same TV ad. "Aiden?" His voice was a little dry, his mind elsewhere, most likely already rummaging around inside Brian's underpants.

"Same again," I said, trying to normalize the heightened atmosphere in the room by sounding everyday.

"Right!" he said as though he was referring to the drinks, giving me all the verbal attention he was able to muster. Lionel spoke just loud enough to hear himself. It helped him focus on his task.

He set about making the drinks. While he busied himself fetching glasses, ice, and unscrewing bottles I took hold of Brian's elbow and pulled him onto my knee, more for my own pleasure than to initiate any work-related sex. Ordinarily this was a little too cute for Brian. Surprisingly he went with it, falling onto me heavily like one of my brothers trying to instigate a play fight. Brian knew how to work a scene with a punter, and I guessed he'd assumed I was up to something. In reality I just liked touching him, not necessarily in a sexual way. And I didn't do myself a disservice by keeping myself part of the show. Simply by placing Brian and myself next to each other physically meant that Lionel would first see the visual of us together, and this in turn would provoke a sexual response. He was a man, after all, and a horny one. As they say, "It ain't rocket science." And I was a good whore. I knew my job and I knew men. More than this, I knew punter mentality.

Once we had our drinks we all began to act more naturally. Still it was *acting* as far as I was concerned. I can't speak for Brian really, but I think I can tell a stage kiss even from a seasoned whore.

Brian kicked off his trainers and pulled his tracksuit bottoms down, and this time Lionel didn't stop him. Underneath Brian wore nothing and his hard dick was already standing at attention. Its disproportion in relation to the world around him surprised me again. (It always did. You'd think I'd remember.) Brian waved its heavy head, and swung around to reveal the sweetest, smoothest bum in London. Again Lionel didn't stop him. He was good like that.

Everything went according to preordained rentboy timing. Generally we knew when each of us would pull which trick out. This evening's performance was pleasant, but it certainly wasn't the greatest show on earth.

This was the third time I was naked like this with Brian and a punter, and once again I knew nothing but body heat would pass between us (and maybe some body fluid, if I got lucky). The obvious reason was that Brian didn't fancy me. But all men are creatures of the here and now, into instant gratification, and rentboys commonly have sex with men they don't fancy. Doing the math, you'd think that Brian and I would have done it by now. Why did he hang around me so much and spend so much time talking to me? Anyway, I expected to leave Lionel's flat more frustrated than when I'd arrived, and appreciating Brian even more—*aesthetically* speaking. No doubt I would wind up jerking off when I got home, to relieve this. As disappointed as I was, I was prepared for what wasn't going to happen. I accepted the inevitable with impressive professionalism.

I was lying on my back on the black-and-white-tile-effect linoleum floor in the kitchen (an old trick—do usual stuff in unusual places; it comes across as new and exciting) while Lionel sucked my dick. To my surprise Brian took hold of my legs. I let him, interested to see where this was heading. He lifted them as though he was going to fuck me. Instead he stuck his beautiful mouth against my bum hole. It seemed sacrilegious but I didn't stop him. The show was the important thing and if I had to make sacrifices for the sake of my art then so be it. As I said, I was a good whore, at times utterly selfless. Besides, it felt fucking amazing.

When it comes to licking bum I'd always rather do than be done but who in god's name would have thought that Brian's perfect-looking mouth also had such talent? I've heard it said that everybody has one thing—a clever brain, an impressive dick, powerful calves, interesting pubic hair, whatever. Brian had more. It wasn't fair. Anyway. Wow! Brian. Bring it on.

In time Lionel moved off my dick to watch what now definitely was the greatest show on earth (at least it felt like it to me).

"I'm going to cum if you don't stop that," I warned Brian a few minutes later.

Brian's beautiful lips pulled away from my bum just long enough to say, "Cum."

The word alone had a physical effect on me.

Lionel endorsed this, saying, "Go for it, fellas."

Apparently I had no option.

Brian plunged his tongue back in, deeper than before, hitting some previously unknown spot—clever boy—and there was no turning back. I started to cum. Because of the position it shot onto my face, with two squirts splashing across my lips. The whore in me thought myself unprofessional for getting so excited that I was unable to hold off longer and provide extra footage for Lionel. This frame of mind quickly changed.

"Me, too!" Brian exclaimed.

Mainly my senses were aware of two things: his pretty white cum on my suntanned abs and the temperature of his cum when it landed.

He fell forward and kissed me. By then I didn't give a damn about how our scene looked to Lionel. This was all for me. Brian kissed my neck with what seemed like genuine passion. Shit! What a hot boy! I was impressed at his professionalism. Who would have guessed he was such a great actor?

For a moment I fantasized that he liked me. Then I stopped myself. All I knew for sure was that I would definitely use him again for three-way work.

Mad Trev

AFTER LEAVING LIONEL'S I HEADED HOME, FIRST making sure to put Brian on the tube and thereby create physical distance between him and *my* punter. It was David's birthday and my plan was to take him to dinner at the Ivy. This would be a double celebration, because just yesterday I'd got back a negative HIV test result. (I hadn't been too worried, but it was still a relief.) The Ivy was, sadly, relatively famous for its usually far too English celebrity clientele. It always had a spattering of fashion self-conscious (but in no way fashionable) gays. (Shit! Was *I* one? In my defense, I was paying with disgusting, filthy, virtually cum-drenched cash, so I had the god-given right to just appreciate their battered cod and chips followed by their celebrated sticky toffee pudding. It would be unfair to call it merely a dessert. When sensational enough, I believe things should have names of their own, like Mick Jagger's lips or Cher's wigs.)

Usually when I'd finished work at the Clinique on Saturday, I'd go home and read for a bit to unwind. This was just one of the ways in which I filled the weird moments between coming up and coming down. Other things I did included running the brothel and servicing at least five private clients a week (that's what they preferred to be called, and why not give them a posh name that was more in keeping with their expenditure). In addition to this I managed to navigate two boyfriends, do laundry, and shop for groceries. Finally I had a part-time, highly lucrative job carrying drugs for Mad Medusa Trev. Like Trev I never carried both money and drugs, but even somebody with the limited intelligence to get into the police force would guess that if I had five hundred E on me I was more than likely selling them. Ordinarily I would carry all the E to Heaven, where Trev and I were now the main dealers. Depending on the night and who was available, I'd give them to about ten to twenty minions to distribute.

I'd just finished Herman Melville's *Moby-Dick* and was starting on John Fowles's *The French Lieutenant's Woman*. After only the first four chapters I knew I was going to like the author's intrusion into his text. He was a more intriguing and far funnier character than those within the plot of the novel. As much as I adored Meryl Streep in the film version it really hadn't done the book justice. I had so little scholastic education that I read constantly in an attempt to fill in the blanks in my knowledge. (I always read paperbacks, making notes in them with a four-color pen. In black ink I underlined clichés and things I thought were badly expressed. I marked brilliant groups of words, sentences, or passages with green bubble shapes that sometimes extended around the whole page. Words used in unexpected or powerful ways I underlined in red. Under words I didn't understand I put a wavy blue line as a reminder to look them up later, so as not to interrupt the flow of my reading too much—unless the sentence made no sense without looking up the meaning immediately. Later I'd highlight the words with a fluorescent marker in my old Oxford dictionary, to help me remember them. I kept the dictionary open at the last word I'd looked up and as I flicked through the pages to find a new word I'd be reminded of the ones

I looked up before.) At worst I'd know what I thought of a few books.

So what, you might say. What use was it in my current line of work? For one thing, I liked reading just for the sake of it. And writing interested me. For another, knowledge of literature might come in handy in the event that a punter actually wanted a conversation with me—improbable but not impossible, as my experiences with Lionel (and Gerrick before him) had demonstrated. In fact, I believe I learned more about the human spirit during one hour with a punter than in all my years at school and all my reading since then.

I'd even go so far as to suggest that being a prostitute should be included in all school curricula (perhaps as part of communications studies). I know this wouldn't be popular with some parents but other parents might approve, as they'd benefit from enjoying their neighbors' sons and daughters. It made sense economically—more kids could afford a good education—and there'd be so many more happy older and ugly people in the world. What perfect universal balance, in a yin-fucks-yang-paying-for-yang-fucking-yin way, with youth and old age thrown into the mix. No doubt the government would ruin the whole idea by taxing it heavily.

I couldn't carry any gear for Trev tonight because David and I planned to meet Hugo after dinner and spend a romantic evening at home. Hugo was working as a waiter in the restaurant at a private club called the Gaucho, and didn't finish work until eleven-thirty.

Before I left the apartment I finished the last of some coke I had, so that I'd be able to cope with Trev. (After all, it was David's birthday and I could always eat dinner "coke-lite" style. It'd work out the same because the tab for the coke would more than make up for skipping a course at the Ivy.) Then I popped in to Trev's flat to remind him I was off duty for the evening and that he'd have to carry his own drugs. But even after doing an epic line of coke I wasn't high enough for Trev's special form of madness. It usually took several E before I could begin to reach even the outskirts of his level of crazy—his looks, random comments, quirky movements, his disappearing in a shifty and arbitrary way and then turning up again and simply being completely wrong while there. So I didn't stay long.

Traditionally David spent the early part of his birthday with his parents in Devon. We'd arranged to meet at eight o'clock. I hailed a cab outside Trev's apartment and asked for Seven Dials, Covent Garden. After just three blocks I heard car tires screeching. My driver jammed on his breaks. This threw me forward in my seat. We skidded to a halt. No crunching of metal against metal. No blood. Two cars were in front of us and one behind, blocking us in.

At a speed I couldn't comprehend, two men dragged me roughly out of the taxi, hooked their arms under my shoulders, hauled me into a back alley, and pushed me into a large garage doorway. I didn't have time to be scared, and definitely had no time to wonder what was happening.

"Drug squad," said one of the men.

Shit! There were so many of them. The one who'd spoken to me looked like a cartoon mug shot of a thug: shaved head, black stubbly face.

"You're fucked, mate," he continued.

All I could come up with was, "But . . ."

A man with a big, hooked nose frisked me while two others pinned me against the doorway. They were only in my peripheral vision, so I couldn't tell much about them except for the fact that they were both bigger than me and there was a strong smell of body odor. I liked it.

"He's clean!" Hooked Nose said, clearly surprised. His accompanying expression made him look comical, like a Shakespearean fool.

"Drop your jeans!" said the shortest of the bunch, a Chinese-looking man in his forties.

This all happened so fast I didn't even think to register if the men were good-looking. The only information I could gather was very basic stuff—color, shape, size. They weren't even wearing uniforms; technically they could have been anybody. We were out of sight from people who might be passing on the nearby street. Still, two men stood together to block any possible onlookers from seeing. This made them seem more like cops, although their clothes confused my eyes with clashing patterns of browns and blues in their shirts and trousers.

"Drop your jeans!" the Chinese-looking one said again with more authority.

I didn't feel in a position to question whether this was legal or not. I wondered if any of them could tell I'd done coke. Even if they couldn't I felt paranoid enough to think they might be able to. I also didn't know whether having cocaine in my system was illegal. If they challenged me about it, the clichéd response would be to suggest that somebody must have spiked my drink. As if anybody would give free cocaine to a complete stranger.

"And your boxers."

I was almost certain this wasn't legal. Any fool would know you couldn't carry a stash of E in boxer shorts. To pack drugs securely you needed briefs, preferably snug, Speedo-style. (Although I was aware that blue was a more flattering color on my Irish skin, I preferred red. I just found it sexier.) Knowing I had no drugs on me, I became bold. The scene already was quite surreal but now that I understood what was going on, time began to decelerate, not just to normal speed but to slow motion. Thumbs either side in the elastic waistband, lingeringly I pulled my boxers down. It was one of those rare and quite magical moments in life when you get stopped by the drug squad, pulled out of a taxi, ordered to strip, and you're really glad you wore a cock ring. If I interpreted his microgestures correctly, I believe the Chinese-looking cop's eyes widened.

"And the back. Turn around."

I knew my bum looked great, as I'd been doing lots of squats and step machine at the gym lately. I wished I had eyes in the back of my head.

"Bend over."

He coughed, I think to fill in some kind of mental space or possibly to punctuate what he said next. By now I found the situation a little amusing.

"Pull your cheeks apart."

I'd never been more glad that I'd let a punter shave my bum hole just two days ago in preparation for licking it. It must have appeared brand-new. The Chinese-looking cop coughed again.

Cartoon Thug turned around. "Anything?" he said.

"He's clean."

With my head bent so I could see past my bum to the cops, I said, "Can I?"

"Sure. Stand up and do yourself up."

When I'd done as he'd suggested he said, "So you know Mr. Keller?"

"Who?"

"Mr. Trevor Keller."

"Oh, Trev. Kind of. I wouldn't say we're close."

"What would you say?"

My fly zipped and button done up, I felt a little more in control. "I know him from the club scene."

"And why exactly were you around there this evening?"

"To tell him I wasn't going to Heaven."

"Why?"

"It's my boyfriend's birthday and we're having dinner."

"And why would you have to tell Mr. Keller?"

"Because he normally puts my name on the guest list. He knows everybody." This much was true. "And I didn't want him wasting my free entry."

"Why didn't you just call him?"

"Why waste a phone call? I have to pass his flat to get a taxi."

There were more questions. My answers in no way incriminated Trev. This is how stupid the conversation was.

"You know he deals drugs?"

"Trev?"

"Surely you've noticed."

"No! You're kidding! Sometimes there's dodgy characters around there but I just assumed they were his mates."

"It's no laughing matter." Suddenly he sounded like a cop. "How did you think he makes a living?"

"He lives in a council flat. He told me he gets unemployment benefits. Apparently he's not fit to work because he's a bit crazy. If you spoke to him you'd know it's completely believable."

After a few more minutes of radio noises and shuffling cops, whiffs of body odor, surprise, and random questions—maybe in an attempt to catch me out—and consistently getting no sense out of me, they let me go. I arrived at Covent Garden a little late. The police went round to Trev's flat and arrested him with the E. He was subsequently sentenced to three years. Thank god it was David's birthday; otherwise it would have been me doing time, not Trev. This was as close as I ever wanted to get to selling drugs again.

Most dealers I've met seem to become blasé after a while. Either that or freaky paranoid (but that's because they're using too much themselves as well as dealing). Either way the cops always catch them eventually. Four people I knew were currently doing time. Some simply disappeared, who knows where? There's a message hidden in there somewhere, I'm sure. Oh, yeah, that's it. Just say no—to *dealing* drugs, not *taking* them.

Danny Cocker

IN INFINITESIMAL WAYS EVERY SNEEZE INFLUENCES your life, but some things stop you, turn you, and push you spinning off in a different direction. Little did I know that I was about to meet somebody who would change my life drastically.

Kinky Gerlinky was the most fabulous club night in the world: extravagant, sensational, decadent, and crazy, a visual bombardment of fabric, color, outlandish personas, and good old-fashioned having a laugh with your mates—all of you in drag. For their last party I'd worn a Minnie Mouse outfit. The gloves and ears were borrowed from my niece Michelle, who had bought them years before at Disney World knowing they'd come in handy someday. Proceeding from the principle that if you're going to do something outlandish you may as well get an expert to help you do it properly, I had a professional do my makeup. I blacked out all my teeth with nail varnish except for the two upper ones at the front. On my way to the club men in passing cars wolf-whistled at me several times.

The Kinky Gerlinky bank holiday party on the twenty-sixth of August 1991 promised to be another exciting evening. How could it be anything but wonderful with performances by Neneh

Cherry, MC Kinky, Boy George, Sonique, Mark Moore, Nina Hagen, Nick Kamen, and Sinéad O'Connor? The name itself promised something extraordinary: *Dazzle Ball*. It was a charity event.

Kinky Gerlinky had been founded two years earlier by Michael Costiff and his wife, the glamorously glimmering Gerlinde Costiff, both of whom were club hosts and general trendsetters. Some credited Kinky Gerlinky as the birthplace of the late Eighties and early Nineties boom in drag culture. Parties were held monthly in the West End. Hugo and David didn't like these types of events so they never went. It didn't matter. I was more than happy to go by myself, as there were always lots of people I knew there.

For tonight's party at the Empire Ballroom I'd decided to go in man drag. As usual I spent the whole day getting ready, although what I finally came up with looked like it took ten minutes to achieve: a pair of boots and black mesh shorts with diamanté wrapped around my balls to act as a cock ring and keep my dick impressive. In the midst of so much overtly feminine fabric and costumery, some of it deliberate travesty, I looked elegantly masculine and—more significant—understated. Over these I wore jeans and a jacket, which I took off in the taxi and stuck in a rucksack so that by the time I arrived I had no problem stepping out practically naked. (It helped that I took an E before leaving my flat.) This meant I could make a remarkable entrance, which after all was half the fun.

The taxi could only get as close as the edge of Leicester Square. Instead of waiting in line, I went to the front. Tasty Tim, one of the DJs, and Roy were on the door. Tasty was wearing a white Afro, a tight beige leather miniskirt, and matching boots. Roy was doing his usual hyper stud with the body of a god, and a short black straight wig swept to the side. "*Gorge*, girl!" they welcomed me, and swept me inside.

The E was quite trippy and by now I loved everything. After a couple of drinks I headed to the bathroom. In the bright lights of the toilets everything—dresses, tights, wigs, lipstick—looked saturated with color. I had to wait for a cubicle. I reclined my head against the wall behind me, closed my eyes, and let myself trip a little. Peeing was going to be an ordeal with my balls so tightly bound.

The noise of a cubicle door opening brought me back to the present, but in no way to reality. Standing in front of me was the devil, wearing only tight red Speedos (my favorite), a pair of horns, and a goatee, with a long, thick, red forked tail hanging down behind him, between his legs (god knows how it was attached). He looked like Fritz, my boy from the YMCA showers, but older, more manly. My tummy flipped. It couldn't be. Could it? I must have jerked off about him hundreds of times in the last few years. From the expression on his face when he saw me, it was clear that it was.

He looked amazing. Instead of stepping out of the cubicle, he took my hand, forcefully pulled me inside with him, and locked the door. Immediately he turned me around, yanked down my shorts, and crouched so that his face was level with my bum. After a three second pause—the waiting nearly killed me—he put his lips against my bum and gently rubbed them back and forth across my crack. Was I imagining this? At that moment I would have sold my soul to this devil if only he'd stick his tongue in my bum. He went one better. He pulled my cheeks apart and with a loud, throaty sound spat a heavy load of saliva in the middle, then stood up and put his dick against my hole at some unreal, trippy speed. The acid in my E might have emphasized this.

In the cold light of day in an STD clinic, I would have said *Let's get a condom, are you negative? Don't put it in.* But this was night in a disco toilet and either I was too high to mind or he was too beautiful to stop. Either way he was rock hard. What more proof did I need that this was right and good? I told myself I believed he was too young to have HIV—the oldest excuse in the book to let a stranger fuck you without a condom. In any case I had no time to rationalize this properly—as if anything would have made me stop him.

His dick, not lubed enough, lunged in awkwardly and staggered in a series of jolts. We both writhed in pleasure. Before I had time to position myself to jerk my dick, he cupped my chin in his hand and pulled my head back. Pressing his hot mouth against my ear he said his first words to me tonight: "I'm cumming." Admittedly they were the sweetest words he could have said after I'd fantasized about him for years. Even better was the sensation of his hot cum squirting up my bum. For the first time in my life I actually felt it inside me. I'd heard rumors of it but never actually felt it before. I'd thought it a gay myth.

We slowed and stopped. He rested his head on my back. I turned around and looked at him. He hadn't even taken his Speedos off.

"Will you pass me some toilet paper, please?" I asked.

"You don't need it. You were clean as a whistle."

"Phew! That wouldn't be a good look in these shorts. They show too much."

"I think they show too little. It's a shame to cover any part of you."

"Surely there's some cum on my bum."

He cupped my bum with his thick hands and felt around the hole.

"No," he said, pleased with himself. "It's all inside. There's just a bit of spit."

He grabbed some toilet paper and gave my bum a quick wipe. I pulled up my shorts.

"I guess that was overdue," I said. "It is Fritz, isn't it?"

"And you're Aiden."

"God! How did you remember?"

"I had a crush on you forever," he said wistfully. He lowered his head and pouted. "Why didn't you call me?"

"I was scared that you were underage."

"What's that got to do with desire?"

"Baby, I argued that point to myself so many times but I just didn't have the guts."

"You could tell I liked you."

"That doesn't make it any more legal." I paused. "But I could call you now. I'm guessing you're old enough."

"I have a boyfriend now."

"Damn. Is he here?"

"He's around somewhere."

"He lets you out of his sight?"

"Listen, I'll give you my number again before I leave and we'll take it from there." He unlocked the cubicle door. "And don't worry, I don't live with my parents anymore."

"Wait one minute, buddy." I turned him around and gave him a long, proper kiss on the lips. "Now *that* was way overdue."

We left the cubicle. My cramped dick was a lot bigger than it had been when I went in. Some figures dragged Fritz off when we reached the dance floor.

Apart from my mum, most of the people in my life seemed to be at Kinky Gerlinky that night. Many of the old Burlington crowd were there. Kydd was in Madonna drag, wearing the pointy bra bustier by Jean-Paul Gaultier. Myles, in a synthetic flowery summer print dress, lipstick, and blusher, looked like an old female version of himself. It was meant to be ironic, I think. The problem was he didn't look different enough from how he normally did. Mark Lawrence never did drag but his friends still called him Mahogany. Even Cubus was there. I don't know who she'd intended to come as, but she looked like Sigourney Weaver's ugly sister.

There were the usual club stars, many of whom could turn out a drag persona as easily as breakfast cereal. Michael Hardy came as Maria Malapasta, who had the look of a Moors murderer serial killer. Champion snogger Jeffrey Hinton was doing a nonspecific somebody off a soap opera. The gorgeous and talented Les Child tonight shone as the sumptuous Manita. Sheila Tequila came as her terrifying yet always-charming self. Bodymap designer David Holah brought Lola Hola, and was quite simply the most beautiful woman in the world. There were also a few in drag that weren't accustomed to it (or even drawn to it), like music video/film director John Maybury, who came as Mary Martyr. Club original Peter Hammond let Space Princess out of her box. Winston was giving it beyond realest of real. The only person doing fierce woman better was the relentlessly stylish Princess Julia. This wasn't simply because she really was a woman but because she was Julia and therefore never less than unbelievably flawless. Leigh Bowery came as himself but also as a toilet complete with seat and lid. Performance artist Nina Silvert came as Lady Godiva, in flesh-color knickers and a knee-length white wig, pulling a pony on wheels behind her with a nose bag handbag dangling from its mouth. She'd sit on the pony and drink cocktails. Adorable.

At one point I spun off the dance floor and saw a man leaning against a podium by himself. He was dressed as an American Indian, with a headdress and skirt made out of feathers. He'd sprayed his skin gold. Something drew me to him.

"Hello," I said. "What are you doing?"

"Nothing."

He had a slightly goofy smile. I sensed he was a bit lonely, and I liked that he didn't hide it.

"Who are you with?"

"Nobody. I'm just a spectator."

There he was again with that humility, honesty, and friendliness.

"No, you're not. You look better than most here."

'Stop it, eh?"

"You're Canadian."

"You spotted the *eh*."

"I love it."

"The name's Danny Cocker but you can just call me Danny. It's easier for the white man's tongue."

I had a soft spot for Canadians but Danny didn't fit the usual mold. He didn't seem to fit any mold. He was new. After only a few minutes talking, he told me he was going to LA the following week to do some porn, and asked me to go with him. He said he'd introduce me to some directors, in particular Chi Chi LaRue.

"You'll love her. She's a scream, and so sharp."

It sounded good. Working at the Clinique had become as mundane as the Burlington, with clerical chores thrown into the mix this time. And what did it say that I was worrying about other rentboys stealing my regular clients? I was ready for a change. Besides, I'd never been to California. But surely I couldn't just pack up and leave London. I had boyfriends to inform, a job to quit, regulars to let down, and sunglasses and shorts to buy.

"Do you like acid?" said Danny.

"Sure."

"Let's do some. We'll have to go the toilets, eh?"

The toilet was a mass of feather boas amid screams of "girl-friend" this and "bitch" that. Luckily not many people were there to pee but mainly be seen in brighter light. Soon Danny and I were in a cubicle.

Danny fished out tabs of acid that he'd tucked into his boot— the most obvious place to hide drugs if you're not wearing jeans with that specially designed little pocket. (I never knew what else it could possibly be used for.)

"I'll have to tear one off," Danny said. "I've got four but it's best to do just one, or a half if you're not used to it."

"Trust me," I said, "I'm quite used to doing drugs."

Considering that he was already fucked up, he tore off a tab with surprising agility.

Outside the cubicle people suddenly started screaming and crashing about.

"Security!" a voice boomed. It sounded more aggressive and loud than usual, more serious.

Danny panicked. Both of us in the toilet looked bad enough, but with drugs . . . He put two tabs in my mouth and two in his own.

"Swallow!" he said.

The obvious thing would have been to flush them down the toilet, but *obvious* has different meanings when you're high. At that moment taking two tabs of acid seemed the most sensible thing to do, so naturally I did. Laughing, as though this might diffuse the situation, we fell out of the door—only to find that *security* was just some queen wanting to pee. Granted, she was thirteen feet tall in heels.

The night unraveled as you might expect on so much acid. Colors got more vivid, moments more intense. Conversations were funnier and everything was more confusing. And then the *Dazzle Ball* was over. Danny and I had lost our coat check tickets. We waited until the end and were ushered onto Leicester Square in the early hours of the morning.

It was snowing. (Well, that's how I remember it, but it's very unlikely, even in London, given that it was the end of August. So I guess it was the acid. Still, that's how it felt. If you've never done acid, believe me it's as good as the real thing when tripping.) We stood like fucked-up kids, without a clue how to get home.

Thankfully clubland's shining, smiling, full-of-love Mark Tyme left the club after us. We only knew each other by face and reputation, yet he saw what a mess we were and rescued us. What a sweet, kind man. I don't remember how we got there but soon we were in his apartment. He put Danny and me in a bedroom to come down however we liked while he went and chilled out with some mates in his living room. All I could comprehend was warmth, soft blankets, and that I was safe.

Chi Chi LaRue

I HAD BUTTERFLIES IN MY STOMACH AS THE PLANE touched down with a thud at LAX a week later. There was no turning back now.

Immigration and baggage went swiftly and smoothly. Usually when arriving somewhere new I breathed in deeply through my nose like an animal checking the scent of new territory. It was also about checking out the new climate and air quality. This might stem from my having grown up in an industrial town and spent summer holidays on my grandparents' farm in Ireland. Despite the overwhelming smell of animal shit, I'd always think, *Ah! Fresh air*. Also I was hoping to leave my mark.

But even before my first proper sniff on the curbside outside passenger arrivals, I noticed the temperature. Heat enveloped my body, at once relaxing and oppressive. I let myself acknowledge the positive aspect. I began to notice smells contained in the heat. They seemed familiar but came in a different mix than I was used to. Car exhaust followed closely by gasoline seemed to account for around thirty percent. Competing with these was a pungent pine disinfectant fighting for recognition with whiffs of cinnamon, coffee, and a mash of other human "enhancing" odors—

hairspray, deodorant, clashing perfumes. It's a wonder there was room for oxygen. I stopped myself before my lungs were anywhere near full, thinking it wise to take shallow breaths until I was outside the airport terminal.

Danny smiled excitedly. He knew this was all new to me and he was introducing me to a new world, or at least a different version of the one I'd known. After leaving the dull weather in London, Los Angeles was paradise. As our cab pulled out of the airport, Danny pointed to the sign over a strip joint. *Nude Nude Nudes* it announced in big colorful letters, as if telling us we were heading in the right direction.

The sky above the pack of hotels surrounding the airport was hot blue and hazy but nothing could taint my thrill. Soon the airport odors were replaced by new, less easily defined smells rushing in at us through the open cab windows. Somewhere I'd heard hot air through car windows compared to a hair dryer. I closed my eyes and gave in to the cliché, and meanwhile checked in on Little Fella to see how he was doing. He felt wonderful, happy to be alive. This gave me a warm sensation in my gut. Then I remembered how much newness I had yet to see. Why waste time now when I could close my eyes tonight when going to sleep?

I opened my eyes and returned to Los Angeles. Turning to face Danny, I found he'd been watching me.

"Sorry," I said.

"Don't be silly, Pooky. I know what you were doing."

"You do?"

"I can't detail your exact version of it, but you were feeling good. Deep down."

"I love you, Danny."

"I love you too, Pooky."

From the first day after we'd met at Kinky Gerlinky Danny

and I had slotted into the groove that would define our relationship: comfortable, intellectually challenging, platonic, playful, and sweet. We often interacted in a familiar, at times silly way, and were always affectionate together. We trusted and believed in each other.

I took in whatever I could from the back seat of a speeding taxi. Mostly it was road signs and other cars behind, in front of, and beside us. But they did have Americans in them, so without being too obvious I peeked at them every now and then. From what I could make out we were on the Santa Monica Freeway. To my right were huge yellow derricks gracefully yet powerfully dipping in and out of the ground, pumping oil as though they were fucking the earth—masculine, western, filmic. This is what I'd left England to see. We looped the freeway and veered onto La Cienega. A signpost read West Hollywood. We passed seedy blocks to ones that were not so seedy with rundown car repair shops. On our left we came to a big department store called the Beverly Center.

The thought of staying in an American motel burned in me, propelling me beyond eagerness into impatience. What would it be like? Far ahead of us to the right I could see the famous HOLLYWOOD sign. It didn't have the elegance of the Chrysler Building in New York or the Gothic mysteriousness of Notre Dame de Paris, but it seemed fitting that LA's most famous landmark was actually spelled out in capital letters—in case you didn't understand immediately where you were. No doubt there was a good reason it was white, although black would have been as striking and more dramatic. TV programs had taught me that Californians liked things easy—language, comfort, humor, getting from A to B and having access to food once there—and something in me wanted to immerse myself in this simplicity and its extremes.

Once we passed the Beverly Center the shops looked more like ones I might actually use. On tree-lined side streets I could see cute little houses that reminded me of the old cartoon *The Flintstones*. We turned off La Cienega onto Santa Monica Boulevard and pulled in behind an International House of Pancakes. Famished, I leaped out of the car and headed towards it.

"Where are you going, Pooky?" Danny said.

"To get my first taste of America, literally."

"Shouldn't we unpack first?"

Then it hit me. We'd arrived at our destination.

The Holloway Motel looked as though it had arrived pre-assembled, not like a house actually built with bricks and mortar. Sure it might be noisy with the traffic from the main road nearby, and yes it might possibly house some dodgy characters, but it was a *real* American motel. Hopefully I'd get used to it and it wouldn't seem so foreign after a while. If I did well during the next few months that it would be my home, I'd become part of all this—Los Angeles.

Enthusiastic as I truly felt, part of me couldn't help cringing at how synthetic everything in our room was. From the gray pile carpet verging on shag to the "paper" on the walls there wasn't a natural fiber in the place apart from what Danny and I were wearing. But the windows were only filthy on the outside and just like in real hotels there were white plastic cups covered in clear plastic and the toilet paper was folded into a V shape. Apparently the maid service did a good job.

Danny lost no time getting us out of the room. We changed into shorts and T-shirts. Then despite the extreme heat we covered six or seven blocks in a short time (Danny always walked at a fast pace). He guided me left off Santa Monica Boulevard onto a quaint street called Wilcox Avenue. On the right-hand side of the street just past the intersection, he turned onto a garden path and led me to a house out of "Hansel and Gretel" where a man opened the door wide. I read this as welcoming.

The man had dyed black hair and wore comfortable, loose-fitting clothes. I knew people like this in London. There's a day-time version of themselves they live in that tells tales of their nighttime glamour: plucked eyebrows, a bit of glitter sparkling on the neck or chin, remnants of makeup around the eyes. (I don't care what makeup-remover ads promise, eyeliner's a bitch to get off. It involves scrubbing away, red eyes, soap, and then more oily wiping. There's no easy, one-step answer.) As surely as she could tell I was a Brit, I knew she was a drag queen.

"Danny!" she screamed.

"Cheesh!"

They dove into a hug. She seemed as pleased to see him as he was her. It looked like there was genuine warmth between them.

She invited me in. "Would you like a soda?" she asked.

"A glass of water would be nice," I said. My mouth was dry—from the walk and nerves. "I'm not used to this heat," I added as an explanation.

"You never get used to it," she said. "It's what we call here, *haawrt* as hell!"

I laughed, not out of nerves but because I found her funny. She wasn't at all intimidating as I'd expected her to be. Her easygoing approach put me at ease.

"So, my name's Larry," she said casually. "But most people call me Chi Chi or Cheesh."

"My name's Aiden."

"Aiden." She looked like she was thinking about the name.

"I've grown to like it," I said.

"It's cute."

"It's the only one I've got."

She laughed. "You're funny, too."

I looked into my glass of water shyly.

"My Pooky's a sweetie, isn't he," said Danny.

"So how long you guys in LA for?" Chi Chi said, looking at me.

"It depends how things go, work-wise," Danny answered.

"Yeah," I said, as though I didn't have a brain of my own. "I don't know."

"Well then, let's get some Polaroids. But for starters, what's your hair like under that hat?"

Like a bashful school kid I pulled the baseball cap off my head. My hair was curly and about an inch long all over. As though it would make it any better, I ran my fingers through it.

"Nice," said Chi Chi. "Let me get my camera."

She took it from a table and returned. For a moment nothing happened.

"You'll have to take you clothes off, Pooky," Danny said.

Before we could go any further Chi Chi had to see the tools of my trade.

"Sorry. I thought Danny would have filled you in," she said.

In random order I removed my boots, then my T-shirt, then my shorts. I stopped at my underpants.

Danny laughed.

"Pooky, you'll have to get naked and get your dick hard, so Cheesh can take a Polaroid."

Nerves kicked in and overtook me. This was my biggest nightmare. She was going to judge whether I was good-looking and hot enough to be in a porn movie. My hands sweated and my legs began to shake. My mouth was so dry I could hardly speak.

"I . . . don't know . . . if . . . I can," I stammered. "Maybe . . . I shouldn't be here."

From the way I was behaving you'd think I was a virgin, and certainly hadn't been a whore for several years now.

Danny sat beside me and put his arm around my shoulder. This only made me notice my nakedness more.

"Who's my little bear?" he said.

Instantly I relaxed. "I am," I said. I softened into him and laughed. Not knowing the proper etiquette for this situation, I said, "Would it be rude to ask to be left alone a minute?" then added, "You know, to get hard?"

Danny was naturally much more exhibitionist than I was, so I think this was new territory for him. He looked up at Chi Chi with a sweet, questioning expression.

Not missing a beat, she said, "Sure! I'll go into the kitchen. Give me a shout when you're ready."

"I'll come with you, Cheesh," said Danny.

I thought it kind of him, but then again they did have a lot of catching up to do.

After about five minutes my dick finally got hard. Thank god for the power of fantasy. My inspiration was the black guy in a snug gray suit who'd sat in front of me on the plane, especially when we had to pass each other in the aisle. My fantasy involved kneeling and licking his butt in the plane's toilet cubicle.

"Hello! I'm ready," I shouted.

Quietly and solemnly Danny and Chi Chi came out of the kitchen, not wanting to scare away my hard-on. Then with complete professionalism Chi Chi stood in front of me and took a Polaroid of my dick.

Flash.

"Profile," she said with military precision.

Flash.

"Now your butt."

Flash.

She could have been flicking through TV channels with a remote control.

She waved the Polaroid in her hand as it developed, then glanced at it.

"My god, you look like Richard Gere."

I couldn't help wondering what spurred this. It was as though she hadn't noticed we looked alike until she saw me naked with a hard-on. Was it a memory?

She showed me the Polaroid. I cringed. There was the scrawny English boy with pale skin I knew so well. I wasn't pumped up in an LA way. My hair wasn't boy-next-door crew cut but wavy, unruly, and shapeless as a teenager's. Nothing about me looked like a porn star.

In spite of this Chi Chi said she would show my picture to all the big porn companies for whom she worked. (She seemed to be involved with most of them. I'd never heard of any of them but Danny had told me they were the most respectable porn companies in the world.) How nice of her. It was obvious she was only doing it because I was a friend of Danny's, so that I wouldn't be embarrassed.

I admired Danny's *I don't give a damn what you, your friends, or anybody thinks* attitude. It was something I recognized, because it was what I'd always been about myself, especially when it came to my own sense of propriety, morality, and behavior. But when it came to my looks I simply felt ridiculous. Mirrors didn't lie, did they? Nobody was fooling anybody. I was what I was, a scrawny, not very good-looking guy who could pull off being sexy because I was intelligent enough to know how to fake it.

"So what shall I say your name is?" Chi Chi asked me.

"Aiden Shaw," I said, a bit confused.

"But that's your real name," she said, as though I'd made a mistake.

"I know. I want to use my real name."

She made a funny face. "Why would you do that?"

"Why wouldn't I?"

She looked puzzled and a bit taken aback. "Maybe some day you might get a job in government and not want people to know you did gay porn movies."

"I never want a job where I'd be ashamed of my life."

I felt as though I could see Chi Chi thinking this through. I suspected that she had seen enough of life to understand what my comment indicated, and perhaps respected it, or at least its boldness. Only time would tell if my decision proved abiding integrity or was simply immature foolhardiness. Perhaps she was too clever to consider all this. In context such issues were hardly in the balance.

After a moment she said, "*Aiden Shaw* works," as though naming something as inconsequential as a shoe insole.

I smiled nervously.

"Why not? It's different," she added encouragingly. "And who knows? It might stick."

When we left, I hoped I'd meet her again, because as Danny had said she was funny and sharp. If we did, I knew it would be as friends. I was certain nothing would come of any of this pornographic movie stuff.

EPILOGUE

As it turned out, I was wrong. I went on to perform in over fifty porn films and became the highest-paid gay male porn star in the world. Some of the best photographers on the planet have photographed me. I've appeared on the covers of countless magazines, many of them having nothing to do with porn. Journalists have been curious enough about me to make me the subject of relentless feature articles and interviews. All this increased my value as an escort. It's shocking how much men were willing to pay me just because I was a porn star.

Along the way I also wrote three novels, two books of poetry, and a memoir. My writing has been anthologized. I've written for literary journals and special-interest magazines about subjects ranging from Levi's jeans to interior design to HIV. With no music experience or training, I wrote and produced two albums as a member of the band Whatever. I even went back to school and got a Masters degree in Creative and Life Writing, despite having dyslexia (discovered when I was tested by the school).

But I continue to believe that life is the greatest teacher. As Aiden Shaw the sexual outlaw (which was how both prostitution and pornography were still thought of by many in the early

Nineties), the body was my textbook. I gained a unique insight into the complex relationship between the observer and the observed. I learned about the function of desire within a market economy—I literally knew my own monetary worth—and developed my own language to articulate a self beyond conventional morality. I scrutinized fans' and customers' behavior, making not just mental notes but putting these thoughts, feelings, responses, and reactions down on paper in poetry, prose, songs, and interviews for other people to judge.

Some boys believed that being paid for sex proved how much punters wanted you. They forgot that being *wanted* is different from being *desired*. *Want* is multilayered and involves the wanted boy and the wanting punter. *Desire* may have nothing to do with the boy—and often did. A psychologist might say that I was looking for attention and that what I really wanted was to feel loved because I had not gotten enough from my parents. I'm certain that some have discovered weirder ways to achieve this than from punters sucking their dicks or fans watching them have sex in movies. It was true that I didn't feel loved enough by my parents, and especially not by my dad—go figure—but this may be only a coincidence and not necessarily the cause of my becoming a prostitute. Some rentboys I met had had suffocating parental love, almost to the point of mania. Maybe that's all *love* ever is, and what I'm doing now is just playing with semantics.

David once asked me to try and recall instances of my mum and dad being affectionate with me when I was young, and I couldn't think of one example. Dad was always at work, as far away from the family as possible, preferably in another country. With seven kids to look after—plus a dog, a cat, and commitments to the church—Mum simply didn't have time for "luxuries" such as showing affection. To her, feeding, sheltering, protecting, and clothing seven of us was sufficient. Many would say what she gave us was enough. But on a profound level, *I* feel it wasn't. Looking back now, I'm not convinced that in her heart of hearts she believed what she gave us was enough. I would ask her, but to get a true answer would entail breaking her heart. Why make her suffer for her mistakes? It's too late to be of any use to me, and I'm not that mean or angry. And I think on some level that I was trying to make up for this lack with material things that the money from prostitution could buy me, and the fleeting adoration that came with the job. Of course I know it doesn't work that way. I can never fill that hole. But what's a guy to do? I can't change the past.

Thinking about my life—the hustling to be paid for sex, on streets in various cities, on porn sets in California surrounded by naked bodies, shooting up crystal meth at some grungy dealer's pad, lying in a hospital ward with some HIV complication—I've asked myself why I did it the way I did, wondering, *Is this what I've become? Is this who I am?* People invariably define themselves by their work: a police officer, a teacher, a dancer. Then who am I? A prostitute? An artist? A writer? An interior designer? An editor? A musician? A student? An academic? Am I trying to discover some true self within all my selves or am I merely a cultural tourist, pretending to be this or that? I recently told an interviewer that I've been completely fucked up by the sex work I've done. I'm as broken as you can possibly get, and don't know if I'll ever be fixed. My current therapist says it's not about *fixing*, it's about seeing it from a different perspective.

I've been in therapy for twenty years, and I've come to believe there's another reason I did porn and prostitution besides *validation*. I was rebelling against morality and Catholicism and everything that I considered to be bad. I broke all the rules of propriety. That was part of the deal. I fought so hard against things I felt were unjust that I hurt myself irrevocably. I took the

Catholicism out of the boy, but not the martyr. I wouldn't want somebody I loved injecting drugs or doing prostitution or doing porn. Not even people I don't care for. But still I did those things. If anybody reading this is thinking of following my example I'd say, be sure it's really you doing it and not a reaction or rebellion to somebody or something. Others will be only too willing to hurt you. Why help them do it? The vast majority of men who want to be porn stars wind up as background, group-sex porn fodder, flesh for quantities' sake whose names no one remembers. So take heed.

Did I sell my innocence for a taste of stardom? I definitely sold my innocence, but what else was I going to do with it at the time? From what was on offer around me, it would have been like throwing pearls to swine. I began sex work in 1986, but the seed of it, the reason I was able to choose it as an option probably got into me way before then, along with all the other mixed-up messages about sex. And although I haven't done punters for years now, sometimes I miss the validation. I miss being flown about to new places. I miss the money. More contradictions.

It's possible that Little Fella saw where I was heading and created Aiden Shaw as armor to protect himself. The facsimile was so good that people believed it was real, and the longer he did it the thicker the skin became and the more it encased Little Fella. I was taunting life, being too fearless. In a desperate attempt to break out, Little Fella may even have made Aiden Shaw lie in the road drunk so that he got run over by a car. It didn't help, because now Little Fella was trapped inside a big, clumsy, paralyzed body, not only of no use to anybody else but no use to himself. I had to relearn how to blink, swallow, and eventually walk again. I think Aiden Shaw was aware of all this and tried to show some of the Little Fella inside him by writing. But the public preferred the bravado, the ornament, the superficial surface of Aiden Shaw. I must have, too, because I went back and made more movies and saw more clients.

So the big question is: Has my dick been the making of me or my ruin? As Gypsy Rose Lee observed, you gotta have a gimmick. My big dick gave me material for my first book and the money to live on while writing it, but I think it was the years of hard work that kept people interested in me. So I'd say it was the making of me. But I've been wrong about other things and I'm definitely not unbiased. In the preface to *My Undoing* I wrote (some thought rather defiantly), "I am not a reformed character and I'm not ashamed of my life so far." I stand by that statement. I'm not reformed. But I am different.

At forty-three years old I've been in and am now out of the porn industry. I'm sitting in Central Park in New York City. It's seven AM. There are joggers and cyclists but not much else besides nature and the skyscrapers peeking over the trees. I feel good. This isn't chemically induced, a high from the night before, and it's not because of cash I earned from selling my body or the fact that doing so made me famous. It's not because I've found true love. Quite the opposite, in fact. I'm not looking for some- body to complete me or make me better. I'm enough as I am. No matter how soft, silly, and stupid I can be, I make myself laugh. Sometimes I smile at my reflection in the mirror and it's not because I'm on antidepressants, it's because I see the irony of me, the mistakes I've made and the successes—and I'm fine with the results.

Although my teacher Miss Bartholomew and others like her made me doubt myself when I was too young to challenge them, ultimately Little Fella was the best teacher I ever knew, when I finally began to listen to him. That dear *is* me—my soul, my con- science, my ability to care about myself—my true nature. And this is precious. Right?

ABOUT THE AUTHOR

Adult film superstar **AIDEN SHAW** is the author of the best-selling memoir *My Undoing: Love in the Thick of Sex, Drugs, Pornography, and Prostitution*, which follows chronologically the events of *Sordid Truths*. He is also the author of three novels, *Brutal*, *Wasted*, and *Boundaries*, as well as a volume of poetry, *If Language at the Same Time Shapes and Distorts Our Ideas and Emotions, How Do We Communicate Love?* Visit him online at www.aidenshaw.com.